Standing in the Sun

AN ODYSSEY OF LOVE, LOSS & SURVIVAL

For Pete,
Special wishes
for your healing!
Nancy Perrini

NANCY BROWN
PERRINI

New
Concord
Press

Standing in the Sun
©2005 Nancy Brown Perrini

ISBN 1-887932-26-7
Library of Congress Control Number: 2005922206

Cover photograph ©Luke Ewing.
Used with permission.

Cover Design: Toni Leland

·Printed in U.S.A.

New Concord Press is an imprint of the Equine Graphics Publishing Group
Zanesville, Ohio

TABLE OF CONTENTS

Preface by Gary H. Quehl, Ph.D. 6
   President Emeritus
   Council of Independent Colleges
   Council for the Advancement & Support of Education

Introduction and Acknowledgments 8

Chapter I - Coming Home...............................11

Chapter II - The Journey 34

Chapter III - Life in Suspension........................56

Chapter IV - A Question of Faith......................88

Chapter V - A Little Miracle........................... 111

Chapter VI - Turning Out the Light............... 137

Chapter VII - The Transformation 149

Epilogue.. 167

About the Author.. 181

*"God stooping down gives us sufficient light
in our darkness to rise by, and I rise."*

⏤Robert Browning

These pages are dedicated

to the memory of the late John Anthony Brown,

to my son, William McClanahan, who shares the memories,

and

to my husband, Nicholas Perrini, whose love and support

enabled this book to come to fruition.

PREFACE

"Oft, in the stilly night,
Ere Slumber's chain has bound me,
Fond Memory brings the light
Of other days around me"
                    –Thomas Moore

May 14, 1979 was a balmy spring day in Washington, D.C., and the cherry blossoms were in their full glory. I felt honored to be among guests of President Jimmy Carter's White House and share in commemorating the twenty-fifth anniversary of the Supreme Court's 1954 decision in Brown v. Board of Education–the landmark that outlawed segregation in the nation's public schools. After President Carter's remarks, we moved to the East Room to mingle, replay experiences, and renew friendships over mint juleps.

"Hello, Dean Quehl," said a black man with the sparkling blue eyes. "I can't believe it's really you." I knew I had seen this fellow before, so I pressed him to help me remember.

"I was one of your students–certainly you recall when we black students held President Brown hostage in the Lindenwood Colleges' library to protest the Vietnam War and racism in America?"

Remember I did. Chris Smith, the Mayor of East St. Louis, shared his memories of those troubled days, and we swapped stories about the legendary leadership of Jack Brown, my mentor and esteemed friend.

John Anthony Brown. In my forty years in American higher education, I have found few college and university presidents who even approximate Jack's magnetic charisma, powerful intellect, and inviting personality. He was an educational innovator without peer, and a bold risk-taker as well. Everything I have come to know about the value and character of small independent colleges is based on principles that I learned first from him.

Jack was truly an accomplished professional. His career included the posts of magazine editor (Time, Inc.); dean of men, assistant professor of international politics, assistant to the president (Temple University); vice president for public affairs and finance (Occidental College); vice president of plans and projects, vice president for academic affairs, and the faculty's choice for president (George Washington University); twice a college president (Lindenwood for seven years, and Muskingum for three); and consultant (the Danforth and Ford foundations and the U.S. Office of Education).

Just as my chance meeting at the White House in 1979 leaps from memory as if it were yesterday, so, too, did that meeting inspire a rush of feelings and recollections about Jack Brown and the wonderful relationship we had enjoyed. It's not only that Jack had the audacity to appoint me as his academic vice president and dean when I was all of twenty-nine years; we also had a warm friendship, which included the delights of fishing, the challenge of debating ideas, the many visits to his beloved Maine coast, and our shared grief during a personal tragedy that happened to one of Jack's sons.

Now, thirty-three years after my Lindenwood experience, and twenty-five years since Jack's death, we are privileged to possess the memoirs of the extraordinary woman who was Jack's wife during the last five years of his life–my colleague and dear friend, Nancy Perrini. Nancy had a distinguished career of her own before retiring, discovering the gift, and having the willingness to write transparently about deeply moving personal experiences. She was Alumnae Director, Acting Dean of Students, and Director of Admissions at Lindenwood–after which she served a marvelous nineteen-year-tenure as Director of Corporate/Foundation Relations at Capital University.

But why should Nancy Perrini's memoir interest anyone who doesn't know Jack or her? Simply this: If we live long enough, each of us will experience the profound grief that comes from personal loss, and the two choices that are before us—either remaining stuck where we are, or transcending tragedy to emerge with both tender memories of a deeply-felt past and the desire to live fully and courageously in the present. Clearly, Nancy elected the choice of embracing life, and all that it brings.

Nancy Perrini invokes moving stories about Jack Brown the man. But there is much more; she whispers sweet memories of their devotion to one another. All of this will warm the hearts of we who continue to remember, and we who love them both.

Gary H. Quehl, President Emeritus
Council of Independent Colleges
Council for Advancement and Support of Education

INTRODUCTION & ACKNOWLEDGMENTS

My dream for *Standing in the Sun, an odyssey of love, loss, and survival* is to connect with readers, ease their pain, enlighten their spirits, and challenge their lives. My hope is to inspire those who face the death of loved ones, and reflect on both the spiritual dimensions surrounding illness, and the difficult health care decisions facing families of the critically ill.

I literally lived in a cardiac intensive care unit (ICU) for thirty days with my husband, from his admission to his sudden and unanticipated death. This book is about that experience; my unusual access to the ICU and those who worked there; and it also provides a positive perspective on patients, families, staff, and hospitals.

In the context of one's lifetime, the journey was a momentary fragment, but the experience was all-consuming. Then suddenly, I was catapulted from a life of great joy into the depths of despair. The pain, the loss, and the grief were incomprehensible. Acceptance and transformation emerged slowly. Beautiful memories and my faith in God and the human spirit gave me the courage to pull myself together, explore new opportunities, and begin again. These pages recall the journey, with all the joys, the sorrows, and the dreams coming full circle.

Had it not been for an observant doctor, these pages might never have been written. A physician from India, Dr. Ganga, stopped me in the hospital corridor one afternoon. He commended me for staying in the ICU, and proceeded to tell me, that in India, when a person is hospitalized, it is required that a family member be with the patient at all times. The Indian philosophy is that family is important to the patient's well being.

Dr. Ganga had been in America for five years, during which he had worked at three hospitals. I was the first non-patient he had observed living in a hospital.

Shortly after our conversation, I decided to keep a log of my extraordinary experience. Years later, I realized it was the scribbled writings which enabled me to detach myself from the situation. I became an observer of the experience, as well as a participant. My written words were the wheels getting me through each day. The yellow legal pad, faded and crumpled with its torn edges and tear-stained pages, contains my writings, clear and legible as the day they were written.

Standing in the Sun recounts how I survived loss, transcended grief, and learned to embrace life once again. It is written with the hope of helping families cope through critical illness and loss of a loved one, and for those who are struggling to get their life back on track. I wish readers the faith, the love, and the audacity to envelope the mystery of life. And, may you enjoy the reading as much as I have savored the writing of these words.

Except for family members and a few professional colleagues, please note: the names of living persons have been changed to protect their privacy.

As *Standing in the Sun* has come to fruition these past five years, I have been blessed with the friendship and support of my writer's group, The Split Infinitives: Sandi Dubin, Lynn Elliott, and Betty Garrett. Their insights, their critical editing, and their laughter have spurred me on.

I will be forever grateful to Gary Quehl for his friendship, and for his willingness to write a preface for this book. A special thanks, also, to my advanced reviewers: Lynda B. Huey, Kurt Keljo, Paula Labita, Becky Martzo and Janice Tucker McCloud, who diligently assisted with archival research. Without my editors, Gretchen Hirsch and Toni Leland at the New Concord Press, these pages would never have become public. My heartfelt appreciation for their subjective critique, suggestions, and many long hours devoted to this project. NBP

Chapter I

COMING HOME

"The final test of a leader is that he leaves behind him
in other men the conviction and the will to carry on."
— *Walter Lippmann*

Two-foot snow drifts glistened in the brilliant morning sun as mourners entered Muskingum College's chapel on a frigid winter day. My eyes, blurred from the light reflected off the snow, barely saw the gaze of a thousand joyless faces as the college basketball team carried the cherrywood coffin down the lengthy flagstone aisle. The young men, usually dressed in crimson and black French shirts and athletic shorts, looked strangely out of place in their ties and dark suits. Except for their shuffling foot steps, the silence in the chapel was riveting.

Dressed in mourning black and gripping the hands of my son, Bill, and stepson David, I slowly followed the casket with its spray of red roses. It was the longest walk of my life, and my internal body was trembling, as if my nervous system had gone haywire. What happened? I thought. What went wrong?

Miraculously, Jack had rebounded, albeit briefly, from a thirty-day journey in a St. Louis hospital. I had made arrangements for us to fly to Tucson, where Jack could recuperate in the warm Arizona sun. Clearly, God had other plans.

Now, our family, the Muskingum College community, and friends from afar were gathered to bury John Anthony Brown: my husband, a dad and stepfather, a college president, mentor, and friend. Was I dreaming, or was this reality? Shocked by the turn of events, I felt like I was having an out-of-body-experience. Surely this was someone else's nightmare, I thought.

My wobbly legs somehow managed to carry me past the sea of faces to the front of the chapel. The family members filing into the first two pews included Jack's daughter, Barbara, from Washington, D.C., where she lived with her husband and two sons. Jack's eldest son, Anthony, with deep blue eyes and thick auburn hair came next. Anthony was married and a hospital administrator with the U.S. Navy. Philip, the middle son, lived in San Diego with his wife, Becky, and Jack's grandchildren, Callie and Tyler. I could hardly look at Philip without crying. Of the three boys, he most resembled his dad. Next was twenty-five-year-old David, a Muskingum student, and his stunning, blond, blue-eyed wife, Katie. David and Katie lived in college rental property only a short distance from the president's house.

Sitting to my right was Bill, who, at six-feet-three, towered over us all, and then, there was me with my dark hair and brown eyes, looking thin and gaunt–I had lost at least ten pounds. In the pew immediately behind us sat my parents. My father, Linwood Alvis, with his bald head, trim figure, and long stride, was approaching his seventy-second birthday. My mother, Esther Elizabeth Neblett Alvis, was a tall vivacious woman with blue-gray eyes and neatly coiffed brown hair, sprinkled with gray.

From the earliest I can remember, Mother was a beautiful woman. Her strength and courage in the face of disaster was an important role model for me. My parents also grieved for my loss. Jack had brought a new perspective and excitement to their world. They would miss him, too.

On that heartbreaking morning, the entire family sat in the uncomfortable pews, looking like stoic robots. We were each lost and alone with our thoughts–missing Jack. The Service of Thanksgiving for the Life of John Anthony Brown was about to begin.

The magnificent pipe organ resonated with Bach's Toccata, and Fugue in D Minor, the composer's genius surely quivering in every heart present. Bach was one of Jack's favorite composers, and the fugue that I had requested was his favorite organ composition.

The organist for the service was our good friend, Nora Abrams. Petite, with warm dancing eyes, Nora's nimble fingers could make a keyboard sing. The powerful majestic sounds reverberated from the organ, rose to the rafters, and vibrated in every crevice and corner of the chapel. The music racked my emotions and I was unable to contain my anger—the tears flowed like an unending river.

With my watery eyes glued to the casket, I visualized Jack rising up to say, "Here am I, send me." He had used those words from Isaiah in his first speech to the college community. My thoughts were lost in my own memories when, suddenly, the music came to an abrupt conclusion. You could have heard a pin drop on the cold stone floor. The stillness was haunting until Edwin Ahrens began to speak.

As I clutched my wet handkerchief, I recalled the tiny piece of paper with the ragged edge containing Jack's message. "Ed Ahrens, Clint Keyes, Brown Chapel." Jack had scribbled those names on a slip of paper and left it on his bedside table for me to find later. I surmised that he knew it was time for him to go. Would I have wanted him to tell me face-to-face? No, probably not, but after his death, I was grateful for the ragged bit of paper with its instructions.

Although Clint Keyes, who had married us, was unable to participate in the funeral service, our good friend, Harold Smithers, Episcopal priest from Augusta, Maine, read the scripture lessons and gave the benediction.

Splendid in its gothic architecture, cathedral ceiling, and stained glass windows, Brown Chapel was named for a former professor. In jest, Jack had always called it "me chapel." It was a fitting tribute for a place filled with recollections of our relationship with the campus community: weekly chapel services, musical/theatrical performances, and distinguished speakers.

There were many notable lecturers during our tenure at Muskingum College, but the day of the funeral brought forth endearing memories of John Glenn–United States Senator, astronaut, and graduate and trustee of Muskingum College.

John Anthony Brown, seventeenth president of Muskingum College, and his wife, Nancy.

I recalled when John was at our home for a luncheon, prior to giving a commencement address. The evening before, it had rained into the early morning hours; therefore, Jack and I did not anticipate that our guests would wander out-of-doors. Thus, the lawn furniture had not been checked for standing water. The rain had stopped, the sun was shining and, unfortunately, several of our guests did decide to venture outside. Senator Glenn, dressed in a navy blue pin-striped suit, surprisingly found himself sitting in a puddle of water. I was totally embarrassed. Luckily, by the time the buffet luncheon was over, John's trousers had dried.

Somewhere in the congregation that sad morning were John and his wife, Annie.

Although my body was present, the details of the service escape me. As I gripped Bill and David's hands, I slumped in my seat. I felt as if my brain was numb from the shock of it all. Years later, I am grateful to have a copy of Ed Ahren's moving eulogy. Ed was a faculty member in the religion department at Muskingum. To this day, his words convey special meaning:

> ...Because of Jack Brown's faith in God, he knew who he was. When a man knows who he is, he is able to make difficult decisions with boldness and grace. He combined gentleness with strength, graciousness with decisiveness, and his identity emerged from this axial trust at the center of his life.

These powerful words of faith and grace have been a guiding light in many troublesome voyages of my life. On that long ago day, the ride to the cemetery was the most formidable journey I could have imagined.

As I followed the pallbearers who carried Jack's body from the warmth of the chapel into the bitter cold air, my eyes were so saturated with tears that I could hardly see the hundreds of students and friends who lined the walkway.

Three Catholic sisters in their black habits and white headdresses briefly caressed my arm as I passed. Jack had served on the board of their hospital, and had also been their patient. They loved him, as did all the others in my path.

As the family departed in the black limousine, we passed the administration building that housed Jack's office and the church where we worshiped on Sundays. It was impossible for me to imagine that his bright spirit, infectious laughter, and penetrating words would no longer be heard in those corridors. Leaving the college behind, the caravan of cars headed west toward the cemetery. Here and there, local residents gaped at the slow-moving procession.

The graveyard was nestled in New Concord's residential community on the western perimeter. It was tiny compared to today's massive cemeteries and memorial parks. The entrance was flanked by two rugged stone pillars that framed a rolling terrain of grasses, family plots, and tombstones.

In the spring and summer, fresh flowers abound, birds sing,

and surrounding trees blossom, but on that icy winter day, the place was barren except for the stone markers rising like monoliths.

As we approached the burial site, the wheels of the car made a crunching sound on the snow-covered gravel. A blue tent had been erected, and chairs for the family were in place. I exited the limousine and, as I did, a cold wind whipped around my legs and I was grateful for my knee-high black boots.

Appalled to think of Jack imprisoned in the frozen, barren earth, I wanted to turn and run the other way. For me, his soul had taken flight the morning we parted. I was certain that his spirit was hovering over the burial ground. Jack was no doubt thinking, "Thank God, I'm free, the mystery is over."

Months later, while going through all of his papers, on the back of a 1968 calendar I found these prophetic words written in Jack's handwriting: "Following death there is the tomb, and on the tomb–Free at last, free at last, thank God Almighty, I'm free at last. Death is the great equalizer; in death we are all equal."

As I gazed through my teardrops at the fresh roses that would freeze when the snow covered casket was lowered into the earth, I remember thinking that he was free, like an angel. My body ached with pain to think of him without me, and me without him. In five short years, we had been blessed with a love that many don't have in a lifetime. As I sat transfixed, shivering from the cold and the wind, I stared into the black hole where Jack's body would be lowered after the brief service.

The shock of seeing his body at the funeral home had permanently engraved itself on my brain. It was as if he were a department store mannequin. His once salt-and-pepper gray hair had turned almost white, and his skin was pasty, like a ghost. The once-strong, angular facial features were diminished by thin hollow cheeks. Had it not been for the dimple in his chin and his demonstrative hands with their long fingers, the body lying before me could have been anyone. I'd leaned forward to kiss his lips one last time, and gently stroke his hands, which were stiff and cold. The vital oxygen and water had left his veins; he was not there.

Jack had joked the day we left for the hospital, "This will be my uniform." And so, I would forever visualize his dress–a blue oxford-cloth shirt and oriental silk tie, a navy wool blazer, and gray flannel slacks.

The graveside service began, with the snow gently falling, and family and friends huddled close to keep warm. The dean and acting president of Muskingum, Rupert Henderson, read a few verses of scripture, followed by selections from a favorite poem by the Middle Eastern philosopher, Tagore:

> ...Let it not be a death but completeness,
> Let love melt into memory and pain into songs.
> Let the flight through the sky be like the folding
> of the wings over the nest.
> Let the last touch of your hands be gentle
> like the flowers of the night...

And so, as Jack's earth-bound life ended, a trumpet in the distance sounded a gentle rendition of *Taps*. Historically played at military funerals, *Taps* began as a revision to the signal for lights out. The twenty-four musical notes were adapted by Union Army General Daniel Butterfield and his brigade in 1862. Various versions of the words and melody live on:

> "Day is done, gone the sun, from the lakes,
>   from the hills, from the sky,
> All is well, safely rest, God is nigh, fading light,
>   dims the sight,
> And a star, gems the sky, gleaming bright from afar,
> drawing nigh,
> Falls the night, thanks and praise for our days,
>   neath the sun,
> Neath the stars, neath the sky, as we go,
>   this we know,
> God is nigh."

After saying our final goodbyes, Anthony, Barbara, David, Katie, Philip, Bill, and I quickly hurried to the waiting limousine for the short ride back to the house. For those few moments, silence reigned–there was nothing more to say. We had lost our best friend and mentor. Later, each of us would come to understand what a significant impact this special man had made on our lives. Most notably, he gave us the audacity to believe in ourselves.

Who was John Anthony Brown?

In a speech entitled, "As an Educator Sees It," given at Muskingum College in 1977, Jack quoted his father, "...education determines how far you can see." Robert Browning would have said, "Ah, but a man's reach should exceed his grasp, or what's a Heaven for."

Jack Brown spent his life reaching for the stars, exceeding his grasp. He was forever searching for a new idea or a new thought that would give him the hook for a speech he was writing. He also reached out to help others in need–to help a student or friends believe in him-or herself. Teaching students to be creative was part of his very essence.

As his father before him, Jack Brown firmly believed, "everyone has to be educated to the limit of his capacity, if he is to live to the fullest possible advantage as a human being."

Jack was born on July 15, 1918 in Harrisburg, Pennsylvania, to parents who had a profound impact in launching his life as an educator. What a shock his impending birth must have been. Old enough to be grandparents, his mother was forty-seven years of age and his father, John, Sr., was fifty-five when their son was born. Jack's sister, Virginia, was fifteen years older, and busy creating her own life before her baby brother was out of diapers.

The family lived in a comfortable, rambling farmhouse on the outskirts of Harrisburg, near old U.S. Route 40 and the intersection of Harrisburg Pike. When Jack was a child, he and his dad often roamed the fields and woods of south central Pennsylvania. Father and son climbed fences and cut through pastures to get to what they called "their woods."

It was difficult for Jack to keep up with his dad, a huge man at six-feet-three-inches, with legs like a giraffe. Trudging through the woods, his dad expounded on the history of the Conococheague Valley at the foot of the Blue Ridge Mountains. There were tales about Johnny Appleseed as he went hunting for wild bear, and stories about Indians who had lived in the area, leaving their mark in the form of arrowheads.

From early childhood, Jack was an avid reader. "During my high school years, I came home after school and read all of John Galsworthy's novels in the hayloft of the barn. I can still hear the rain on the galvanized tin roof; I can still smell the barn with all its seasonal fragrances; and I can remember how I built, in my own mind, the characters in Galsworthy's stories, using my own imagination and staging their lives with considerable freedom." This tale always makes me grateful that I was given the opportunity to experience Jack's creative mind.

When he wasn't reading in the barn, Jack often helped his mother in the kitchen after school. During the depression years, in an effort to help with the family's finances, his mother opened their home as a roadside inn, attracting travelers from across the country as they traversed old Route 40.

Mrs. Brown hired a wonderful southern cook, Cora, to assist in the kitchen. Cora was a plump, sassy woman with a great sense of humor. She kept Jack entertained for hours, and also endowed him with a love for food and cooking.

His mother's little black cookbook, containing recipes in her own handwriting, was their guide. Now quite old and worn–the binding is loose and the small lined, ragged pages are turning brown–the recipes warm the heart and satisfy the hunger.

One must know how to cook to use this small book. It lists all the ingredients, but it doesn't always tell you what to do with them. Noted below are two favorites:

Lemon Sponge Pie

5 egg yolks
6 tablespoons of butter
2 cups of sugar
2 lemons, juice and grated rind
6 tablespoons of flour
2 cups of milk
Add beaten egg whites
Bake in slow oven on one crust

Curried Fish en Casserole

1 can of tuna or salmon
1 cup cooked peas
Pour over the following sauce:
2 tablespoons of olive oil
2 tablespoons of flour
1 pint of stock
2 small finely cut onions
1 teaspoon curry powder
1 tablespoon mild vinegar
Pinch of salt

Stir constantly till it boils. Cover top with layer of steamed rice, cook in moderate oven for one-half hour, dust grated cheese over top and brown.

Other recipes give instructions for curing meat, making quince honey, *dandelion and elderberry wine, and a chili sauce recipe that calls for eighteen tomatoes. Food was evidently not as highly spiced in those days, for the chili con carne recipe requires, "only enough chili powder to equal a grain of rice."*

Since his mother's cookbook didn't always tell him what to do with the ingredients, when Jack cooked, he used the estimation system–never measured, just guessed. As a teenager, when Jack wasn't studying he spent many hours in the kitchen, watching his mother and Cora, until a serious illness intervened.

During his third year in high school, he was struck with a severe case of viral pneumonia. He developed empyema, whereby fluid from his lungs invaded the pleural cavity, and surgery was necessary. He was hospitalized for many months and missed two years of school; a tutor helped him with his schoolwork. When he wasn't studying, cooking became his therapy.

His tenacity and love of learning enabled him to complete high school and enroll at Temple University in Philadelphia, where he majored in history and political science. He excelled as a leader, and was president of the student government, the debate society, the history honor society, and president of the senior class. The day after Jack graduated; he went on the staff of the president of Temple University.

Several years later, he went to work for TIME magazine's editorial department, and completed his master's degree in international law and politics from the University of Chicago. Later, after completing post-graduate work at Princeton and Columbia Universities, Jack engaged in research under a grant from the Ford Foundation, and also taught at Princeton's Woodrow Wilson School of Public and International Affairs.

Upon completion of his work with Ford and Princeton, Jack returned to his alma mater, where he was appointed dean of men and assistant professor of international politics. Continuing his rise in academe, three years later, he was appointed assistant to the president.

During this period, Jack married his first wife, Franceline, a native Philadelphian and they raised four children together. He and his family enjoyed life in historic Philadelphia. Jack became involved in civic work for the community, campaigned for mayor one year, and cemented many life-long friendships.

Two special friends come to mind: Jerome Armentrout and Furman J. Finck. They would both eventually become my friends, as well. Jerome Armentrout reminded me of George Burns, minus the cigar. He was small in stature and always had a twinkle in his eyes. Jerry, as he was called by his friends, stayed trim by walking five miles round-trip each day from his home in Washington Square to his uptown New York office, where he managed funds for a private foundation.

When Jack and I were in New York, we would take a cab to the Armentrouts' home, enjoy one of Jerry's martinis, and then walk to Chinatown to dine at BoBo's. Since they didn't take reservations, there was usually a long line of people streaming out the door and down the street. BoBo's was a small place with perhaps a dozen tables. The food was served family style—all you could eat for five dollars. It was the best bargain in Manhattan, and worth every minute of the wait. I can still taste their succulent butterfly shrimp.

Years later, Jerry and his wife, Elisa, a quiet petite woman, retired and moved to their native Illinois. World travelers, gardeners, and genealogists, occasionally their trips bring them to Ohio. I feel enriched to count them among my friends.

Regrettably, I will not see Dr. Furman Finck again until it is my time to pass to the other side. When he and Jack first became friends, Furman was a member of the faculty at the Tyler School of Fine Arts in Philadelphia. Later, he moved to New York City where he became a renowned portrait painter. After Jack and I married, we often visited Furman and his wife, Mildred, at their Central Park West home. The dining room with its north-easterly light was Furman's portrait studio, and Mildred's piano studio was an immense room at the opposite end of the apartment.

By the time I became acquainted with the Fincks, Furman's once flowing black hair had turned snow-white. He exercised his trim physique every day. His face was highlighted by his dancing eyes, dark bushy eyebrows, and a carefully manicured white mustache. A wispy little woman with auburn hair, worn in a bun, Mildred was a talented pianist, composer, and a gracious hostess.

For her guests, Mildred shopped at her favorite neighborhood markets for the freshest fruits, vegetables, and meats she could find. Whether or not her company had returned from their day's adventures, at five o'clock sharp, the cocktail hour commenced.

The Fincks were an intellectually stimulating couple with a wide scope of interests in the theater, music, and the arts. They seldom stayed home more than one or two nights a week. If Jack and I were visiting, either friends were invited in for an intimate dinner party, or we went to an art exhibit followed by dinner at the Player's Club. Furman often said, "The secret of a long life is to keep moving." And that he did.

After a long and productive life painting such notables as Helen Hayes and President Dwight Eisenhower, in 1999 at the age of ninety-five, Furman passed on—Mildred had died a year earlier. She'd always worn a beautiful cape, shawl, or scarf around her head and shoulders. I treasure one of her wool scarves that Furman mailed to me after her death.

Until his death, Furman continued painting portraits and teaching at the National Academy of Design. I hope there are paint brushes in heaven, for he certainly must need them. What a role model, mentor, and friend he was for almost a century. I miss Furman and Mildred—their vibrancy, kindness, and compassion touched all those who knew them.

These treasured friends, along with Jack's leadership at Temple University were pivotal to launching his successful marriage with higher education. His distinguished career took him from the east coast to southern California, to the nation's capitol city, and then to the Midwest.

In 1960 Jack and his family left their native Pennsylvania to travel to suburban Los Angeles, where Jack assumed his position as vice president for public affairs and finance at Occidental College, a small liberal arts institution.

Having honed his skills in writing and public affairs at TIME magazine, while in California, Jack created an award-winning public affairs program entitled "Governments of Man," which aired on CBS radio and over the Armed Forces radio network. During the half-hour weekly broadcast, Jack had the opportunity to discuss ideas and current issues in subjects ranging from Thomas Jefferson to China and from ancient Greece to Cuba.

Jack thrived on ideas and doing the impossible. Delivering an address in 1963, he remarked:

> Life at a college or university is so exciting. We deal with ideas which have to do with freedom—freedom from fear, freedom from superstition, freedom from bigotry and bias, freedom from not-knowing. And not-knowing enough about the ideas, the framework, and the system which comprises our free society; not-knowing can be our downfall. In this age it is dangerous not to know, even in the short run, and fatal not to know for long. Our colleges and universities are our best weapon against ignorance, our best attack against emotionalism.

A born teacher and leader, he was a sought-after public speaker, an avid writer, and lover of the visual arts and symphonic music. As if he were a conductor, cuing up the strings of an orchestra, he had a rare talent for eloquently conveying the most penetrating words. I am sure that Jack could not have envisioned life without the spoken or written word–it would have been unimaginable.

With his passion for language, new ways of thinking, solving problems, and challenging the status quo, he delighted in rattling his adversaries with the hope of changing their mindset. He also loved to play the devil's advocate, and thrived on the banter exchanged at faculty meetings.

By every measure, Jack was an iconoclast who impacted the lives of thousands. They were friends from all walks of life: students, colleagues, bricklayers, farmers, politicians, world leaders, taxi drivers, teachers, construction crews, and well drillers, and they were scattered across the country from Maine to California.

After three years at Occidental College, Jack was appointed vice president of plans and projects at The George Washington University (GW), in Washington, D.C. The family returned to the east coast and settled in Maryland.

With new access to the great minds and ideas in the nation's capitol, the "Governments of Man" program continued with CBS Radio. Lyndon B. Johnson was president at the time. Jack was a staunch Republican, so the Johnson presidency didn't always resonate with his beliefs. However, the excitement of the political atmosphere gave him discourse for his speeches and writings.

There is an old family story Jack loved to tell about being Republican: "...when I was born, my father rushed down the hospital corridor to the telephone. His first call was to his Republican committeeman. There was very little I could do about this premature affiliation with a political party. Recently, I have come to doubt the wisdom of my father's impetuous action. He should have given me six weeks to think it over."

As a political scientist, Jack thrived on the excitement of the nation's capitol and his stature at GW multiplied. He was eventually appointed vice president for academic affairs. From all reports, faculty and students alike loved him. "John Anthony Brown has been lauded by the faculty for attracting top quality scholars… and has been idolized by the students."

In 1965, he was the faculty's final choice for the presidency of GW. Unfortunately, the board of trustees had already selected their candidate. On the other hand, had the selection for the presidency been in Jack's favor, he and I would never have met and this story could not be told.

The presidential squabble between faculty and trustees attracted the interest of the media and brought Jack to the attention of a small Missouri college. Several months later, he was appointed president of Lindenwood

College, a liberal arts institution for women. And thus, it was on the banks of the Missouri River in historic St. Charles, that our lives became inseparably entwined.

Twelve years later, John Anthony Brown, my mentor and best friend, was gone, but he would forever reside deep in my heart.

After the short drive from the cemetery, Jack's children, Bill, and I departed the funeral home's limousine, and entered the house through the kitchen door. We were greeted by Maggie, our housekeeper, with tears streaming down her face. Maggie was a tall thin woman with shortly-cropped gray hair and piercing, deep-set dark eyes. She had been raised in the country and lived in the small town of Norwich. Her wants and needs were simple, and her heart overflowed with generosity. She always went the extra mile to be helpful. What a godsend she was for our family.

And then, there was Margaret Richert, better known as Peg. An alumna of the college, Peg had returned to live in New Concord after her husband died. A petite, dignified lady with neatly coiffed white hair and always elegantly dressed, Peg was the official campus hostess. I don't know what I would have done without her guidance.

After hugging both women, I quickly surveyed the kitchen and dining room before our guests arrived. The silverware looked as if it had just been polished, the dishes reflected the light of the overhead chandelier, and the tables overflowed with home-cooked food.

The generosity of the community was beyond belief. Although I had grown up in a small town, I had never before experienced anything like the outpouring of love in New Concord, Ohio. It was a never-ending stream of goodness and bounty.

The tables overflowed with casseroles, a cooked turkey, a whole-sliced ham, numerous varieties of salads, homemade pies, brownies, cookies, the list went on and on. Bill was salivating at the sight, and had already swiped a chocolate chip cookie.

Shortly before two o'clock, friends descended like a flock of geese arriving home. There were students and faculty, friends from surrounding farms, towns, and villages, as well as colleagues from across Ohio and the nation. The line assembled seemed endless. Although my feet were killing me, my hands were limp, and my face was stained with tears, I listened as each person shared a special memory.

First, there was Joe, the basketball coach–one of the gentlest, most caring men I've ever met. One by one, the entire basketball team followed. Next was Mark, with his dark curly hair and muscular physique, a student on the summer paint crew who would eventually become a teacher. Following Mark was Jack's assistant, Gay Whitaker, and her husband, Reeb, both professors and concert pianists. Jeff, the dean of students, always had a twinkle in his eyes.

Next in line were two of my favorite trustees: Jane Stern, an alumna, who had captivated our hearts, and Mary Ann Arthur who had become a trustee because of her high regard for Jack. Mary Ann and her husband, Bill, would continue to be in and out of my life for many years. Next appeared Nick, the young man who'd sat in his cut-offs on the steps of Brown Chapel and talked with Jack about his hopes and dreams. Jack wrote about Nick in his weekly newspaper column for *The Daily Jeffersonian*, Cambridge, Ohio:

> ...I have a lot of confidence in the boy who sat in his French undershirt on the steps of Brown Chapel at Muskingum College. He had torn-off jeans, no shoes, and seemed to be staring into space. Next year he'll be at a top-notch medical school where he hopes to get both a Ph.D. and M.D. He's a good student and a leader among men at twenty-two. Many years ago, on the cornerstone of the building at which he was staring, in print too small for him to see across the quadrangle, was inscribed the following words: "Put off thy shoes from off thy feet, for the place where on thou standest is holy ground."

The motto of that story is: Don't let the undershirt or the bare feet distort your appraisal of today's young people.

Following Nick was Ben, the builder of our retreat house. He moved to his own time-clock, but the finished product was perfection. Then, Sam, a professor who shared the same birthday with Jack, gave me a hug.

Years later, Sam reminded me that Jack had given him an unusual gift, one that was always good for a laugh–a coffee mug with the handle inside the cup. It was designed to be a tribute to

Sam's Polish ancestry. Where Jack had found that mug escapes me, but it was probably at some barn sale or flea market. Twenty-five years later, Sam still chuckles about his gift.

As the long line continued, I was greeted by Victor, a medical doctor and violinist who played in the college orchestra. A particularly memorable character was Louie, a flamboyant art professor who always wore a black cape. Following Louie came one of our favorite students, Sophia, a vivacious Greek girl with olive skin and dancing eyes that were filled with tears that day.

And finally there was Karl, who in Jack's mind was the epitome of the ideal student. Karl would later write me the most moving and profound letter that I have ever been privileged to receive. In part it said:

> "I've been quite hesitant about writing you, and now that I am, I wish I had the efficacy of your husband's syntax. For some reason Dr. Brown picked me to represent the ideal Muskingum student. For me, your husband represents the ideal leader. More than that, I respect and idealize him the way I do my father. Together, Dr. Brown with his charisma and you with your graciousness, you gave Muskingum a new fresh style of self-confidence. You both made me quite proud to be part of it.
>
> When such a man dies, it isn't for us to wish him back nor should we carry a torch bearing his name in order to accomplish what we were unable to do before. I will tuck President Brown's memory inside my head where he will silently correct the angle of my direction. He is up there with my family, my friends, and my experiences. There he will continue to exist until I die, whereupon he will pass to another mind and live there in a continuum, still guiding and influencing."

I have often wondered where Karl is, and what great things he has accomplished. I have never forgotten his poignant thoughts and words in tribute to Jack.

When I thought the long lines had finally dispersed and I could put my feet up, in walks Peter Merrimon, a recent consultant to Muskingum's public relations office, and Garrison Howard, our friend and former dean of Lindenwood College.

During the time Peter had been assisting the college, he had taken an apartment in New Concord, so we saw him frequently. However, the consultancy had come to an end shortly before Jack became ill, and Peter had returned to his home in Washington.

Although I had talked with Peter from the hospital in St. Louis, it had been several months since I had seen him. He greeted me with a warm hug, but his eyes conveyed deep sadness.

Garrison, with his wind-blown white hair and tears showering his face, had burst into the funeral home the previous afternoon. I recall rushing into his outstretched arms as students, friends, and family looked on. I could almost feel his pain and deep sorrow as his questioning eyes looked deep into mine. What on earth happened, he wanted to know.

I had no answers, because the doctor had not, as yet, shared the results of the autopsy report. Eventually, I would learn that Jack's arteries were clear, but the heart muscle tissue had vanished, completely disintegrated, as if it had blown away.

Garrison loved Jack like a son loves a father. Although in recent years Jack and I had not seen Garrison as often as we might have liked, we shared mutual affection, as if he were a member of our family.

I was pleased that Peter and Garrison had come for Jack's funeral. They were so much a part of our family that, had they been absent, something would have been amiss.

After what seemed like hours of greeting friends and being on my feet with no relief, I removed my boots and collapsed on a chair by the fire. The logs were ablaze and the wood crackled. Mother brought me a plate of food, and Peter fixed me a dry martini with a lemon twist. I thought about how Jack preferred olives in his martinis. He liked the salt, while I preferred the refreshing citrus flavor.

Into the late afternoon and early evening hours, I reminisced with Garrison, Peter, and my family. The conversation around the roaring fire was non stop. Heartbroken as I was, it was a memorable sharing of stories, pictures, laughter, and sadness. Although I was emotionally and physically fatigued beyond comprehension, I didn't want the evening to end. I did not want to be alone.

On the other hand, I was not alone. My constant companion was a girl named Charlie, our lovable black cat, named by Bill in honor of his favorite cartoon character, Charlie Brown. Charlie had not let me out of her sight since I'd returned home. While she probably wondered where Jack was, she was no doubt ecstatic to have me to herself.

Hours later, with Charlie curled at my feet and the house finally quiet; I tried to sleep, to no avail. The bed was too empty and my heart was heavy with pain. The tears saturated the pillow as they flowed. As I tried to find a dry spot, I thought about the days preceding the funeral the haunting experience of selecting a casket, planning a funeral from long distance, and coping for hours with the endless line of friends and students who flooded the mortuary to pay their respects.

Unbeknownst to anyone, had it not been for Jack's valium, I might have gone out-of-control. There were so many people surrounding me that I felt as if I were a fish in a glass aquarium with no place to escape, except my mind, but the dark crevices there were not a good place to hide, either.

I attempted to sleep that first night at home, but all kinds of strange and unhinged thoughts flowed through my head. My heart, and probably my brain, was shattered like a million pieces of glass. I didn't know who I was or where I was going.

Where would Bill and I live? What was I going to do with my life? I knew that my parents and Bill's father would want us to return to St. Louis, but as Thomas Wolfe once said, "You can't go home again." I firmly believed that famous quotation, and knew St. Louis was not the answer. Damn it, Jack, why did you die? I cried.

After tossing and turning for what seemed like hours, I switched on the light, put on my terry cloth robe, and quietly crept past Bill's bedroom door and down the back staircase. I fixed myself another drink. I preferred spirits to Valium and was determined not to get hooked on drugs. I had told myself that when Jack's Valium prescription ran out, that would be it. I would not have it refilled.

The first floor of the house was absolutely silent except for Charlie lapping milk from her bowl. I poured a glass of bourbon on the rocks, filled a dish with peanuts, and returned to my lonely bedroom. I lit a cigarette and curled up in a lounge chair with Charlie and Colleen McCullough's book, *The Thornbirds*. During Jack's last days, we had shared the beautiful, but tragic love story of Meggie and Father Brussart. As I read that night, I could almost feel Jack's presence–I know he was there–I wanted to reach out and touch him.

While the pain, the loss, and the grief were overwhelming, I knew my faith in God, and the man I loved, would be guiding my journey in the days ahead. Finally, I slept. The next morning, with my dark circles and blood shot eyes, and by the grace of

God, I began the step-by-step process of taking one day at a time. It would be more like one step forward and two steps back.

The first step was immediate. Shortly after arising and eating a hasty breakfast, my parents left for the long, eight-hour drive to their home in St. Louis. They knew I had things to take care of with Jack's kids and besides, my dad never stayed anywhere longer than three days–it had already been four days. They promised to return at a later date. Anthony, Barbara, and Philip also needed to return to their families.

We all sat in the study that morning and read Jack's will, but I don't remember anything about the discussion. Any monies the children might have received were in the form of an insurance policy, of which their mother was the beneficiary. Jack had not planned to die, or I'm sure he would have set aside funds for Barbara and the boys. I'm sure they were disappointed that I was the beneficiary of Jack's pension fund, but no animosity was expressed, for which I was grateful. I encouraged them to take whatever furniture, paintings, or other items which had special meaning for them.

The boys were interested in several pieces of art work, their dad's clothing, some furniture, and a few memorable artifacts. Anthony selected his dad's antique pine desk and high back chair, reminiscent of the Benjamin Franklin era, and an oil painting by a Polish artist. Anthony was also the beneficiary of his father's silver-initialed ring. Philip decided on the antique grandfather clock.

Barbara wanted her dad's antique goblets, several watch holders, and the baby grand piano. Twenty-five years have passed, the piano has been enjoyed by many in my living room, and the goblets are still stored in my garage. Perhaps, someday Barbara will call and claim what is rightfully hers.

I took what remained, including a few inkwells that were special to me, several oil paintings, an antique ladder-back chair, and a contemporary painting by Paul Jenkins that will some day belong to David's sons.

It was a difficult, but necessary day. Within twenty-four hours of their dad's funeral, they had made arrangements for shipping the furniture. We all said our goodbyes, and David drove his siblings to the Columbus airport. Bill and I were alone at last, but not for long.

After eating some of the delicious leftovers, Bill and I walked through the snow to the John Glenn Gymnasium to watch the college basketball team in action. It was a beautiful starlit night with a full moon reflecting our shadows as we walked across the campus. I thought to myself, "Jack's up there somewhere."

What team the Muskies played that evening, I do not recall. I only knew it was where I was supposed to be. In three years, Jack and I had never missed a home game. But that evening I felt strange, as if I was not of my own body, or part of me was missing. It was extremely difficult to come face-to-face with acquaintances expressing their sorrow. I was numb from the shocked state I was in–talking was difficult and my voice quivered. I was just there, surrounded by the warmth of the crowd.

Suddenly, I realized my body was bone-tired, overcome with exhaustion. The previous month had taken its toll. Like Rip Van Winkle, I just needed to sleep for a long time.

And sleep I did, many nights as long as ten hours or more. Bill let the dog out each morning before he went to school, so there was no need for me to get up. Some mornings were too painful to even think about getting dressed, so I would lie frozen under the covers until the phone or doorbell rang.

Over the ensuing months, I got lots of rest and slowly dealt with the shock, denial, grief, and anger. While my days were busy writing thank you notes, in response to hundreds of heart-wrenching letters and gifts to the John Anthony Brown Endowed Scholarship Fund, I was in a trance most of the time.

Grief was my constant companion, as were the tears that flowed unannounced. The empty sadness was indescribable. In some sense, I was relieved Jack's pain was over; he had suffered too long. On the other hand, I had stretched myself physically and mentally to the edge of the cliff and some days felt like a victim of a major disaster.

My relationship with Jack had been essential to my life, my work, and central to my every thought. Now he was gone. What was I to do and where was I to go? Fortunately, at the invitation of the board of trustees, we were able to live in the president's house until Bill graduated from John Glenn High School that June.

The storms of winter passed and the green coat of spring arrived with the fragrance of lilac bushes perfuming the countryside. Long overdue, Bill and I spent weekends visiting Ohio colleges. His final selection was Miami University in Oxford, where he enrolled the following January.

When not visiting colleges, I drove the six miles from home to our country retreat, most every day. There was no time to sit around feeling sorry for myself. I worked with Ben, our builder, and the finishing touches were added to the cottage; a two-car garage was built as well. What was to have been a retreat house, became our permanent residence.

When I wasn't at the farm, I continued to be immersed in the life of the college and, at the same time, I sorted and labeled items to move or put in storage. I helped Jack's secretary, Karla, pack his personal memorabilia. Poor Karla, she missed Jack, too. A tall woman with radiant auburn hair and dazzling green eyes, Karla was so impressed with Jack's language skills that she had labeled him the man with the silver tongue. Karla and other friends showered us with affection, constantly assisting with the packing of boxes or making sure Bill and I had enough to eat.

I didn't do much cooking that spring, for it seemed Bill and I were always invited to someone's home for dinner. Bill had a special treat when Muskingum's basketball coach invited him to the NCAA final championship game—a treasured lifetime memory.

When we were home, David and Katie often shared a meal with us, either at our place or their apartment. David had difficulty coping with his father's death. Since moving to New Concord, he and his dad had grown very close. David would forever treasure their time together. His dad and Muskingum College had helped him get his life back on track; he would graduate the following year.

As if he were a sheep lost from its mother–in this case his father–some days after class David would stop in for coffee. He and I, and sometimes Bill, sat in the corner booth of the kitchen and reminisced for hours, cherishing long ago moments.

In the midst of all that was going on, one day a cadre of student leaders came to call. They asked if I would consider succeeding my husband as president. Needless to say, I was shocked, but nevertheless flattered. Somehow, they thought Jack's spirit would live on if I were their leader. While confident in my administrative skills, I knew my academic credentials had not prepared me for such a challenge. I knew the students' proposal would not be accepted by the board of trustees, because I did not have a Ph.D. or the necessary experience. Instinctively, I also knew the time had come to sprout my own wings.

It was one of those defining moments. I declined the students' generous and affectionate offer. They accepted my decision with understanding, love, and concern. Never have I felt such a genuine, caring empathy from young people whom I barely knew.

The accolades went on. In early April, student leaders again came to see me. They had collected twenty-five hundred dollars and wanted to have Jack's portrait painted so he would be remembered along with other former Muskingum presidents. Did I know of a portrait painter? I was overjoyed. Furman Finck was the perfect artist.

Almost immediately, I picked up the telephone and placed a call to Furman. He considered the invitation a great honor and accepted without a moment's hesitation. Although he normally received thousands of dollars for his portraits, Furman wanted to paint his old friend, regardless of funds which had been raised by the students.

Within a few weeks, I gathered together pictures and snapshots then flew to New York to spend a weekend with the Fincks. Over the course of the next year, I made numerous visits to New York to view the work in progress. The Fincks soon became two of my closest friends.

When Garrison Howard was appointed to Muskingum College's Board of Trustees, I was again ecstatic, knowing Jack's legacy would live on. Just as Garrison had always been there for Jack, in the future, he would be there for me, as well.

And then, as if that wasn't sufficient recognition, the senior class invited me to participate in their commencement:

> The senior class officers would like to extend our invitation to you to be the honorary marshal at our commencement exercises on May twenty-first. Realizing your great influence on our lives at Muskingum, many seniors have overwhelmingly requested that you participate in this great event of our lives. We would feel honored to have a person of your great rapport with us in our last few hours at Muskingum College. We're anxiously awaiting your response.

The rays of a spectacular summer sun shone brightly as the senior class processed across the outdoor platform on the quadrangle adjacent to the John Glenn Gymnasium. I could almost feel Jack's presence, as students–many with tears flowing–hugged me after receiving their diploma. In my heart, their expression of warmth, generosity, and love elevated Muskingum College to a higher level. I shall never forget them.

Leaving was difficult. Despite the prodding of my parents and friends who wanted us to move to St. Louis or Washington, Bill and I concluded we would move to the cottage on Peach Lane. Why else had we built the house? Had it been otherwise, Bill and I would have been homeless. Besides, our Arabian mare was due to foal in early summer.

On a quiet country lane, surrounded by fourteen acres of pasture, woods, and hay fields, I would get my life back together. With Jack's audacious spirit as my guide, my glorious memories, and my unwavering faith in God's world, life would lead me in new directions, fulfilling my own destiny.

Like a mighty oak plucked out of the universe, when summer came, Jack Brown's withered body was at peace, and his soul was free as the winter's whirling snow or a summer's gentle rain. His spirit would live on in the lives that he'd touched.

Jack and Nancy Brown

**Written by Dr. David Sturtevant
and adopted by the
Muskingum College Faculty
March 15, 1978.**

John Anthony Brown led Muskingum College for less than a thousand days. Interrupted tragically in mid-passage, his presidency ended too soon and too abruptly to be properly assessed. He brought, nevertheless, special qualities to this place: fresh insights from a long and versatile career in higher education; a commitment to curricular and administrative change; and an optimistic dedication to build anew on old yet firm foundations. As a transitional figure in Muskingum's history, he sought effective designs for the future. Still emerging at his untimely death, their final forms will never be known.

If his presidency was too brief to evaluate, his appealing human qualities left a lasting mark. Above all, he was a rational and civilized man. Literate, articulate, a lover of fine music and art, a delightful conversationalist who enjoyed good talk and good company, he presided over Muskingum with warmth, humor, and grace. Together Jack and Nancy Brown restored hospitality and intellectuality to the Manse. Between them, they transformed the vacant old house into both a home and a vital center for campus life. On his arrival in New Concord he complimented the college community on its atmosphere of essential civility. His gracious leadership made a fundamental contribution to the continuation of that humane tradition.

His visions for the future might not be realized, but his intelligence, his charm, and his infectious faith in tomorrow will not be forgotten. In a multitude of ways, John Anthony Brown will be missed.

Muskingum College Bulletin, Spring 1978, page 5.

Chapter II

THE JOURNEY

"Clearly life to him was no brief candle, but
rather a splendid torch to be waved about lustily."
—*Professor Deidre Vakalis*

Day 1

Clutching his chest with one hand and his stomach with the other, Jack Brown gasped for breath and staggered out of the bathroom. Startled, and with a deep-seated feeling of panic, I rushed to him as all one hundred eighty pounds fell into my outstretched arms. Like a river breaking its banks, streams of perspiration poured from his body to mine; his heart rate accelerated alarmingly. With all the energy I could muster, I somehow managed to get him to the living room sofa. Later, I wondered how I did it, but when life hangs in the balance, I am convinced you don't ask how or why. You do whatever must be done.

I screamed up the staircase for Bill to call our family physician, Harry Blain. Jack was in extreme danger and I feared he would die before my eyes. I knew Jack was a warrior and, above all, a survivor. He knew what it was to be critically ill and to face the prospect of death. Thirty-nine years before, when he'd been a teenager, he was struck with a severe viral pneumonia that spread from his lungs and caused the infected fluid to accumulate in the pleural cavity; the doctors were not sure he would survive. Looking at him that day, I prayed that he could again outrun the doctors' predictions.

In 1973, two years before accepting the presidency of Muskingum College in New Concord, Ohio, Jack was diagnosed with cardiomyopathy—an inflammation of the heart muscle that inhibits the pumping of blood, causing irregular heart beats, and slow degeneration of the muscle tissue. Dr. Paul Rainey, a noted St. Louis cardiologist and Jack's physician, thought his disease was probably a result of the earlier viral infection.

Until the fall of 1977, Jack enjoyed every day to the fullest. For him, each hour was a blank page to be filled with stimulating ideas and activities, exciting places, and interesting people. In late September of that year, we drove to Columbus for a meeting with the Ohio Foundation of Independent Colleges, an organization of Ohio private college presidents. Following the luncheon and before returning home, we stopped at our favorite department store.

As we stepped onto the escalator, Jack suddenly broke out in a cold sweat. Perspiration dripped from every pore. His pulse was rapid and his breathing labored. Departing the automated stairs, we found a bench nearby. Jack felt nauseous, so I asked a sales clerk for a glass of water. Jack's pulse rate slowed and he regained composure after taking a nitroglycerin tablet.

Until that moment on the escalator, our spirits were high with the excitement of a new academic year, and the near completion of our cottage in the country. Before heading back to the college, we had planned to shop for a new suit for Jack, a dress for me, and then enjoy dinner in downtown Columbus. Instead, I took Jack's arm and quietly said, "Let's go home."

As I drove east on Interstate 70, we listened to music, and discussed whether or not to call Dr. Rainey or find an Ohio cardiologist. By the time we arrived home, there was no question in our minds; we immediately called Paul Rainey in St. Louis. The doctor was concerned when Jack described his symptoms, and he urged us to fly to St. Louis for further assessment. We left the next morning.

Following three days of testing at St. Luke's Hospital, Dr. Rainey told Jack he could return to work, albeit at a slower pace. Since there was some evidence that the cardiomyopathy had progressed, the doctor sent Jack home armed with new medications. But telling Jack to slow down was like asking a horse that was already streaking toward the finish line to stop and return to the starting gate.

October was filled with football games, homecoming, and a meeting of the board of trustees. During the homecoming parade, we had a momentary scare when the horse pulling our carriage decided to bolt. Adventure lovers at heart, we clung to each other and laughed as the horse galloped away at full speed. Fortunately, a block or so later a Good Samaritan came to our aid.

In November, Jack agreed to undertake an accreditation review of St. Lawrence University in upstate New York. The president of St. Lawrence was a lifelong friend, so there was no way Jack wasn't going to live up to his commitment. In retrospect, I believe he was testing the waters to see if he could resume his presidency at full throttle. Like a teenager asserting his independence, Jack refused to let me accompany him to St. Lawrence.

I was furious; wondering what would happen if he became ill during the trip.

Because I insisted he not go alone, his assistant, Lewis Gary, volunteered to be his driver. With Lewis's assistance, Jack rose to the occasion, meeting with faculty and administrators and preparing his evaluation of the university.

Several weeks after his return from New York, his heart began to fibrillate again, and he couldn't get enough air into his lungs. Back to the hospital we went, this time closer to home. Harry Blain referred Jack to a cardiologist in Zanesville, Dr. Dan Carver, who promptly checked him into Good Samaritan Hospital. As a member of the board of directors of that institution, Jack was comfortable there.

With his balding head, pudgy physique, and down-home style, Dr. Carver was professional, an experienced cardiologist, and very likeable. The care Jack received at Good Sam was exceptional. For two weeks, I spent my days and nights running back and forth between the hospital and the college, a thirty-minute drive each way. Two days after Christmas, Jack was released from the hospital, accompanied by his new friend, an oxygen tank.

Though our celebration had been delayed, Christmas in 1977 brought joy and happiness to our family. My parents arrived from St. Louis, and Bill, David, and Katie brought warmth and laughter to our hearts.

Decorating the president's house was a challenge. Armed with a chain saw borrowed from the campus physical plant, David and Bill plowed their way through the snow-covered countryside, in search of the perfect ten-foot pine tree, Jack's favorite. As a young boy, cutting the Christmas tree each year with his father had been an all-day experience. Finding the right tree wasn't easy, for they never cut a tree with a future.

The goal was a beautifully shaped tree, so situated that it could not possibly grow into a mighty pine. Jack was in awe of their majesty, and often wrote about pine trees. During his confinement with pneumonia as a youth, he spent a lot of time writing poetry.

> *"Wind through the tall pine, always sighing,*
> *Wave pounding the beach rock, never tiring,*
> *Tireless waterfall, rumbling forever,*
> *Mystic star, marching your predestined path,*
> *But tell me, wind, wave, rumbling fall, and star,*
> *What drives you on, what power from afar?*
> *What power but God could guide a star?"*

That Christmas, Bill and David lugged the tall pine home in the back of Bill's pickup truck, and placed it in a stand between the double French doors of the spacious living room. There were barely enough lights and ornaments, and no one had the energy or motivation to go shopping for more. In order to attach my treasured silver angel on the topmost branch, we had to cut six inches from the tree. Shining ever so brightly, the aluminum angel with her curly hair had been hand-tooled by my mother, and I had treasured it since my childhood. Now, reflected on the pale gold wallpaper, the light from the angel gave a warm glow to the ambience of the room.

At that moment, I silently thanked God for bringing Jack safely home, never dreaming that it might be his last Christmas with us.

The centerpiece of our holiday feast was a twenty-five pound turkey. Since I was preoccupied with Jack and his well being, Christmas dinner would not have been possible without my mother's cooking expertise in the kitchen. Famous for her home-made crescent rolls, she prepared most of the trimmings, while Katie and I assisted. Mother fixed her special cornbread dressing, southern corn pudding, mashed sweet potatoes topped with slightly browned marshmallows, cranberry sauce, and lemon chess pie, a favorite family recipe passed down for generations.

A specialty was Spanish beans, a recipe inherited from a family friend. For this quick and simple dish, I sautéed onions, bacon, and green peppers; blended them with seasoned tomato soup; poured the mixture over green beans; and baked the dish for an hour.

Jack and I had inherited a love of cooking and entertaining from our mothers, and ever since our marriage, we had shared fun times in the kitchen, preparing for family and our guests.

In Jack's culinary domain, turkey divan was a favorite. Made with left-over turkey and covered with fresh or frozen broccoli, the dish was crowned with Jack's own secret blend of melted cheeses, mayonnaise, and herbs. Several days following Christmas, Jack was in good spirits and felt like cooking. His turkey divan lived up to all expectations and was again a triumph. I learned to recreate Jack's specialty, but it has never tasted quite the same.

Although our hearts were burdened with worry, we were surrounded by the joy of good food, family, and friends in a place and time we would never forget. Our college home was called "The Manse" because early presidents of the college had been Presbyterian ministers and, historically, their homes were called manses.

A large, rambling, two-story brick house built on a hill early in the twentieth century, The Manse had spectacular twelve-foot ceilings. Three sets of French doors opened on to a veranda from the living room, and a brick fireplace graced the opposite corner. A crackling fire burned on most of the holidays, and into the cold month of January. Many an evening, we all huddled together on the love seats surrounding the fireplace. Originally covered in Chinese silk, the matching sofas had nearly been destroyed by our cat, Charlie. Before moving to Muskingum, we had Charlie's claws removed, and then we recovered the sofas in a Williamsburg crewel fabric.

The Manse

The living room in The Manse could have been a ballroom, or even a basketball court. Upon our arrival at the college three years before, our first initiative was to repaint and wallpaper, lay new carpet, and hang fresh draperies in the living room, adjacent sun porch, dining room, and study. A massive undertaking, but the completed project was stunning. The walls were transformed from drab beige to a pale sunlight gold complemented with ivory gold-threaded draperies. The old rugs were replaced with plush, thick-piled sea green carpet that flowed through the entire first floor.

Arranged in several conversational groupings, the furnishings were a mixture of yours, mine, and ours. A twelve-foot sofa belonging to the college was reupholstered in a gold embossed pattern. Greeting guests in front of that sofa was a favorite past time for our menagerie–Sandy, our collie, Patrick, a mixed breed, and, of course, Charlie. Like criminal investigators, they sat at attention, scrutinizing all guests, until we arrived. Since people in New Concord never locked their doors, this scenario occurred frequently. We wondered how our pets might have reacted to a stranger taking the silverware, china, or stealing some of our art work.

For years before we met, Jack had been an avid art collector. His eclectic personality was dramatically reflected in his selection of paintings–everything from impressionism to surrealism to eighteenth century lithographs. Bringing the otherwise conservative living room to life, the watercolors and oil paintings attracted conversation. One in particular–an acrylic abstract with intense, bright colors flowing towards the center–was exotic and sensual. The method used was simply to roll the acrylics on canvas; no brushes were involved. The painting was a gift from the artist, Paul Jenkins, who lives and works in New York and Paris.

In contrast to the colorful abstract, a Mendjinsky oil painting from the impressionist period hung over the fireplace, and scattered throughout the house were several Andrew Wyeth prints, an eighteenth century lithograph, and a pen-and-ink sketch by Salvatore Dali. As Jack contemplated our home that Christmas, I'm sure his paintings brought memories flooding into his consciousness. I remember thinking that I would love to have been able to read the perplexing melodies dancing through his brain.

Because of Jack's lack of energy and continual need for oxygen, we moved our bedroom to the downstairs study, where a large bay window filtered the early morning sun on the grass-colored carpet. When coming to see the president, students and faculty often entered through the study door that led to the veranda circling the front of the house. The room was a comfortable space for conversation, featuring two overstuffed, wine-colored chairs, Jack's teakwood desk, and a library lamp with a green hat.

On the north, the room was banked by an entire wall of shelves. Filled with hundreds of our books, it was also a showcase for our collections: my pewter, and Jack's inkwells and pocket watch holders, including two antique Staffordshire china watch holders. We rearranged the furniture to accommodate the guest room bed. The oxygen tank huddled ominously in the nearby corner.

Without the additional air for his lungs, my husband was drained of all energy. The tubes were anathema to Jack's way of life. Until that time, he had been an energetic, vibrant human being. "Clearly, life to him was no brief candle, but rather a kind of splendid torch to be waved about lustily," wrote a colleague following his death.

Jack had genuine charisma. There was a magnetism about him that radiated like an aura. When he entered a room, without uttering a word, people felt his presence. Executing each second of every day with passion and vigor, he taught me the importance of making every moment count. Spontaneity was his motto.

Although each day at the college brimmed over with activities, it was not unusual for Jack to call me on the spur of the moment. "What are you doing for lunch? Let's pack a picnic and go to the farm." We'd sold a summer cabin in Maine, and were building a small retreat cottage on fourteen acres, six miles from the college. Watching the little house take shape was a favorite pastime.

Our dream cottage was a modified replica of the John Bracken House in Williamsburg, Virginia. We had carefully researched and designed our plans from the gutters to the floor boards. Unlike today's traditional concept of gutters, in nineteenth century Williamsburg homes, bricks were placed on the ground, side-by-side, directly under where the rain flowed from the roof, the theory being that the water would splash off the bricks and return to nurture the earth. This style of gutter also eliminated the need for cleaning.

Eager to make our cottage as authentic as possible, we purchased cherry wood flooring that had originally graced a one hundred year old house in New Concord. The eighteen inch cherry planks surrounded the massive fireplace, and spread through the living room, kitchen, and small den. The walk-in fireplace held a wrought iron crane (an antique that we had brought back from Maine) and a charred black soup kettle.

While the house was in progress—and when Jack wasn't talking with students, making speeches, or cultivating alumni—he loved to sit on the stone foundation of our cottage and talk with Ben, the contractor, or with Bill and his friend, Doug, who were cleaning bricks for the chimney.

The previous summer, we had hired Bill and Doug to search Muskingum and Guernsey counties for dismantled brick houses. Like scavengers, they combed the back country roads, loading bricks into Bill's pickup truck. Sometimes they purchased old bricks and, other times, owners were happy to have them carted away. Accumulating more than 7,000 bricks was back-breaking and tedious work.

With chisels and hammers, they spent their days meticulously cleaning bricks in preparation for the construction of the massive two-and-a-half-story chimney. After a long, hot and boring summer, the boys completed their job by the time school started.

One of the most thrilling things that happened during the summer of 1977 was searching for water on our property. "When you are building a house in the country, free advice showers upon you like a tropical monsoon." The husband of our cleaning lady, Maggie, told us that it would be foolish to have a well dug without having the site witched. In New England they call it dousing.

Taking a branch shaped like a Y from any tree, peach or elm are preferred, hold the switch horizontal and the switch will move downward towards the site if there is water there. It's obviously an old superstition, but what did we have to lose. It worked! On the second try water gushed at sixty-feet below ground surface. We were able to see it from light reflected off of a small mirror lowered deep into the hole. We would now have *crystal clear, cold water running from our faucets.*

And then, our small plot of land in the hills of southeastern Ohio became our escape hatch from the college. Living in the middle of the campus offered no privacy. Yet, while we loved to slip away to the country, at the same time, we had an infectious love for the college and were committed to its students and faculty.

From Jack's perspective, the college was in a budgetary crisis, and he thought it might be necessary to cut programs and personnel. Later, I would be reminded of Jack's first speech to the college community—a truly prophetic statement: "Thank God we came to grips with these problems while I'm alive. I don't want anybody else to do it, and neither do you."

Sick as he was on that cold January afternoon, in the first scene of this passage, Jack was determined to talk with his chief administrators, who had no idea of the seriousness of his illness. One by one, they came—the dean, the chief financial officer, and the vice president of development.

Jack was committed to moving Muskingum College in the right direction and it was not humanly possible to change his determination. His admirable dedication was of grave concern to David, Bill, and me. While Jack was an astute politician at handling such situations, it tore at his guts and, of course, adversely affected his heart muscle. I didn't dream that the emotional impact of the afternoon's conversations would lead to the emergency call to our family physician.

❧ ❧ ❧

By the time Dr. Blain arrived, Jack was in severe distress with abdominal pain, chest pressure, perspiration, increased heart rate, and shortness of breath. The infusion of oxygen had ceased to be effective. Blain treated him with a diuretic and Valium to lower his blood pressure, and recommended we take the earliest flight to Jack's cardiologist in St. Louis. The doctor was emphatic about not returning to the local hospital, which was filled with patients suffering from the flu, an illness that could be detrimental to Jack's condition.

For the next hour, I was on the phone, making plane reservations, requesting oxygen on board, and placing a call to Dr. Rainey, alerting him to our scheduled arrival that evening. He promised to send an ambulance to meet us at the gate. Suddenly feeling nervous and apprehensive, I escaped upstairs to pack, leaving Jack in the care of Bill, David, and Katie. I was alone and far from the ears of my family; the tears gushed over my face and down my body. Meanwhile, my unfocused and fearful mind flittered from one thing to another, like a bird without a wing.

What in the world was I to pack when I didn't know how long we would be gone? What about cash for the trip? It was Sunday and banks were closed (there were no ATMs in 1978.) Would our pregnant mare survive in the cold foot-deep snow? How were we ever to write Jack's newspaper column that was due the next day?

As I gazed out our bedroom window over the rolling hills, the sunlight danced on the newly fallen snow, and I could see the south window in Jack's office. We had spent three joyous years at this wonderful college. How could we ever leave this place, with its warmth and friendships?

During our first year, we had opened our home and our hearts to nearly three thousand students, faculty, staff, and alumni. An awesome undertaking, but we loved every luncheon, dinner, and reception, particularly the fireside chats and spaghetti dinners with freshman students each year. We'd also traveled thousands of miles, meeting with alumni from the east coast to southern California, and dining with board members in Duxbury, Massachusetts, Bloomfield Hills, Michigan, and on the banks of the Connecticut River. Whatever happened, I knew we would treasure our many friends, and a part of us would forever remain at Muskingum College and with the tiny village of New Concord. Friendships are forever.

Then, my mind returned to reality and, like a lost kitten looking for its mother, I was scared. I prayed out loud, "Oh, God, heal Jack if you can. I'll do what I can, but the outcome is all in your hands." Since childhood, I had prayed to God when I needed somebody to listen. I trusted that my faith and my guardian angel–who is always there–would see me through the crisis.

Suddenly, there was no more time to ponder what had been, or what might be in store for the future. I quickly splashed warm water on my tear-stained face, put on my make-up, and called Karla, Jack's secretary, and Maggie Champ, an angel from heaven. Maggie came to the house three days a week to clean, do laundry, iron, and help me get the house ready for entertaining. Her son, Jock, and my son were both on the John Glenn High School basketball team. She promised to check in with Bill frequently, assuring me he would have clean clothes and food to eat.

After packing a few slacks, sweaters, skirt, jacket, one dress, and underwear, I hurried downstairs with Jack's clothes, shaving kit, clean pajamas, and a bathrobe. His velour-hooded robe made him look like a cloistered monk, but it was soft to the touch, giving a feel of elegance. Thank God the medication had relieved his pain and breathing difficulties. With Bill, David, and Katie to buoy his spirits, Jack was in a more cheerful mood. David and Katie had moved to Ohio the previous year, and we loved having them as part of our lives.

David & Katie Brown, their wedding in the Manse.

After tussling over conflicting values during David's adolescent years, father and son had finally been able to enjoy quality time together. The previous spring, we had hosted David and Katie's wedding in the living room where Jack now lay ill. Weak as he was, Jack was giving the boys and Katie instructions as to what he expected in our absence.

I would learn later that Bill and David had been lecturing him about resigning the presidency. They wanted their dad and step-dad around for a long time. No matter what the circumstances, I knew Jack would never give up the life he loved. When the time came for his life to be over, Jack would "die with his boots on."

By the time the ambulance arrived, the winter sun had set in the distant horizon. Thin and pale in his charcoal grey topcoat, Jack looked proud in his black Russian fur hat. Wearing his favorite navy blue blazer, grey flannel slacks, a blue oxford cloth shirt, and a tie I had made for him, he said, "This will be my uniform."

Parting from our children was extremely difficult. We did not know what lay ahead, but I was confident our lives were in God's hands. Bill, David, and Katie had each other for support. Later, I would dream about Bill, Patrick, and Charlie wandering around the big house alone. Regrettably, our collie, Sandy, had disappeared from our lives following a football game the previous year. During the game we'd chained her to a stake in the yard. We were told that she was stolen by students from another college, but it was never confirmed, and we were unable to find her. The family all missed Sandy, and so did Muskingum's students.

Bill and David assured us they would take care of everything. The responsibility for a house which was on loan must have been overwhelming for Bill. We had no choice but to show him our confidence. (He exceeded all expectations, and I was one proud mother.) I promised to call when we arrived in St. Louis. I really don't remember if I did it, though. It was early the next morning before I could leave Jack's side.

As if we were going off to war, there were tears, hugs, and kisses, and Jack saluted as the stretcher carried him to the waiting ambulance. With heavy snow falling and low visibility, the ride to Port Columbus was longer than usual. In addition to the driver, we were accompanied by a lovely nurse from the local hospital. Marline was a short stocky woman with cascading red hair. Our conversation was limited, but I do recall she had piercing green eyes and a lovely smile.

Jack slept, clutching my hand, and I stared out the window, praying for his body to heal, and for God to give me strength for the minutes, hours, and days ahead. I was afraid, but I was confident our faith and our love for each other would enable us to overcome any obstacles.

The ambulance felt like a cocoon carrying us through the winter storm to a safer place. The brilliance of the full moon reflected on the windows, and snow flakes glimmered like dancing angel wings. Radiating its light, the moon energized my very being. Years later, I would come to understand this energy to be what the Chinese call "chi," but, on that night's ride, the force of light took me back to the day, twelve years before, when Jack and I first met.

The memories remained vivid. Like an entrancing rhythm, there'd been a subtle, psychic synergy between us, yet anything other than a professional relationship had been the farthest thought from our minds.

In September 1966, John Anthony Brown was appointed president of

Lindenwood College, a liberal arts institution for women, located in historic St. Charles. An easterner by birth, Dr. Brown initially appeared out of place in the conservative Midwest, but his infectious personality soon won the hearts of the campus community. He spent his first few months getting acquainted, interviewing each faculty and staff member individually. As a 1956 graduate of the college and a newcomer to the staff, I had been appointed alumnae director, two months preceding his arrival.

On a brisk fall day, with the sun streaming in the southwest window of the president's office, Jack and I sat facing each other in front of his spacious desk. Of course, at that time, I called him Dr. Brown. Except for a brass lamp with its black shade, several antique ink wells, and a glass paper weight sitting on a stack of papers, the desk was bare. With his long fingers knitted together under his chin and his elbows propped on his knees, he and I talked for what seemed like hours. The conversation ranged from his vision for the college to my plans for the alumnae association to our families. His blue-gray eyes danced when he talked and sparkled when he laughed; they never left my face. I sensed he knew my every thought, almost as if he could look into my brain.

Jack Brown was a tall, distinguished-looking man, six feet in height, with a receding hair line of salt-and-pepper gray, a strong, angular face and dimpled chin, like Kirk Douglas. His hands were almost twice the size of mine and had long fingers, except for the right index finger, once smashed in a car door. The finger was slightly bent above the last joint. On the fourth finger of the right hand, he wore a silver ring chiseled with the initial "B," a gift from Anthony, his eldest son. His hands were expressive, conveying a sense of power.

He was an intelligent, charming conversationalist, with a wide expanse of cultural interests, and a keen knowledge of history and world events. At the same time, he appeared to enjoy simple everyday things. I had never met anyone quite like him, this man who was destined to become my teacher, my mentor, and my best friend.

"When the student is ready, the teacher will appear," says Dr. Caroline Myss, author of "Anatomy of the Spirit." In this phrase, she expresses her belief in the power of energy–the force of God–in determining when we meet people in our lives. Somehow, it's always at the right time. Never will I forget that first meeting. Years later, Jack said he fell in love with me on that autumn afternoon.

During Jack's inaugural year at Lindenwood, he was handed a charge by the trustees: to bring male students into the previously all-female student population. What an awesome challenge. Many faculty, staff, and *students were initially uncomfortable with the idea, but in his diplomatic way Jack was able to convince the constituency that if the college were to survive, enrollment would have to increase, and the only way to do that was to become a coeducational institution.*

With Jack's assistance, my job was to convince my alumnae board that, with the addition of men students, Lindenwood could–and would–survive. The all-women board eventually was persuaded, but not all the members were enthusiastically accepting.

In the meantime, the dean of students announced her retirement. My job as alumnae director was full-time, however, after some arm twisting, the president also appointed me acting dean of students for a year.

The first year with men students was difficult, but great fun. The females swarmed, and the once rather subdued women's college came alive with excitement and intrigue.

What a responsibility, and what a year! Having a liberal arts background, I quickly adapted, but I knew absolutely nothing about being a dean. Thank heavens the previous dean, Mary Lichliter, still lived in the community. During her thirty-year tenure, parents sent their children to women's colleges to be protected; in loco parentis was the norm. Mary was a surrogate mother for many students during my college years; now, she was my mentor and supportive friend.

Most days, I flew by the seat of my pants. My natural tendency to have faith in others sometimes got me into trouble. For example, when a young woman (assisted by four of her friends) aborted her four-month fetus in a dormitory toilet, it didn't come to my attention until some four weeks later. Initially, I was told about the tragedy by one of the participants, who happened to work in my office. She was distraught, felt terribly guilty, and could no longer hide the truth.

Upon receiving this shocking information, I told the student that it was my responsibility to tell President Brown, which I did immediately. He summoned Garrison Howard, the academic dean. After recovering from the appalling news, we planned a strategy together. We knew we needed to act quickly, before word reached the campus community and beyond. Long into the night, the three of us met with the students involved, first as a group, and then individually.

Except for the young woman who worked in my office, they refused to accept the fact that their behavior was unacceptable in the eyes of the law, as well as the college community. The young woman who had aborted the fetus expressed no remorse. After meeting with the students, President Brown personally called all their parents, who arrived at the college the next day. After another round of tearful and heartfelt discussions with shocked parents and students, Jack regretfully announced his decision on behalf of the college.

The mother of the aborted baby was expelled, and the remaining four students were suspended for the rest of the semester. Jack, Garrison, and I were exhausted, but knew our decision was the right one for the students, for the college, and for our own integrity. The tragic incident, and our response to it, bonded us for life.

This unfortunate episode played havoc with my emotions; abortion was contrary to my belief system. I was forced to face the changing morality of a younger generation.

Life marched on, and the spring rains washed the remaining debris from the unsettling events of winter. The bright morning sun filtered through the trees lining the campus walkways, the flowering dogwoods bloomed, and May Day was observed in its splendor. By the time Commencement rolled around, a casual observer never would have known what turmoil had transpired earlier. It was a year of professional growth that would be forever enshrined in my soul.

Many times, Jack and Garrison conveyed their gratitude for the way I'd carried out my responsibilities. I felt they respected me as their colleague. When they asked me to accept a full-time appointment as dean of students, I was confounded, but also flattered. Nevertheless, without a moment's hesitation, I declined their offer. To have accepted would have meant graduate school during the summer, and with my family, I simply couldn't make another commitment. (After raising a son, pursuing my career, and serving as the wife of a college president, ten years would pass before I could pursue my dream of graduate school.)

While I missed working with students, I was relieved to concentrate on the alumni association. As my organizational skills continued to develop, I thrived on my work and came to realize my talent for college administration.

The following year, the admissions director resigned, and Jack and Garrison laid another challenge at my doorstep. I was again asked to step to the plate in an interim capacity. It turned out to be a significant challenge—to reverse a declining enrollment. I knew nothing about college admissions, but I believed in Lindenwood, knew the quality of the faculty, and was confident I could sell the academic program to students and parents. My alma mater was an exciting place to be, and I felt privileged to be part of a professional team and growing institution.

Expanding the admissions staff to four assistant directors, three of *whom were alumni, we laid out a plan to cultivate and recruit students. By year two, recruiting initiatives were successful and, to my surprise, President Brown appointed me full-time director. I loved the challenge, the opportunity it provided to help my alma mater and the personal satisfaction I derived from my staff's success. By the end of my tenure, three years later, Lindenwood's enrollment had achieved a significant increase in new students, both men and women.*

But as my career accelerated, my marriage fell apart. Except for the love we shared for our son, my husband, Sid, and I had little in common. We had grown in divergent ways, each having different needs and aspirations; we no longer danced to the same rhythm.

I wondered what had happened to our dream of growing old together. We no doubt loved each other, but like rose petals dropping in the summer sun, our marriage had withered and died. Although the divorce was amicable and Bill saw his dad when he wished, it was a disruptive time. Bill was confused and perplexed, and our families were upset, as well. Telling my mother and dad was difficult, because I was the first in our family to be divorced.

On the other side of the family, my father-in-law, Sidney B. McClanahan, a St. Louis attorney, knew we did not have money for legal fees and offered to handle our case. On the fateful morning of December 7, 1970, the anniversary of Pearl Harbor, I arrived alone at the St. Louis County Court House. Sid chose not to be present. Not believing in alimony, I accepted only child support and the privilege to live in our home as long as I desired. Upon sale of the property, proceeds would be equally divided. I was happy with the agreement.

When the proceedings were final, I gave my handsome, former father-in-law a kiss on the cheek and left the courtroom for the cool, crisp December air. Standing in the sun with the brilliant rays washing over my face, I felt free as the birds perched on the courthouse roof. At the same time, I was sad for my son, and regretted my marriage had ended.

A new chapter in my life was launched, and that was scary at the age of thirty-six. Pointing my teal-blue Volkswagen bug in a northwesterly direction, thirty minutes later, I crossed the Missouri River and returned to my office. Descending like a flock of geese, my colleagues checked to make sure I had survived. With a chuckle, I told them I was a free woman.

While my life had been in a state of upheaval and transformation, Jack's marriage of twenty-five years had also crumbled. And to make matters worse, his eldest son, Anthony, was in an automobile accident, leaving him in a coma for a number of trying weeks. Fortunately, he slowly recovered, but it was a difficult period in the Brown household.

The separation and divorce were tumultuous. The boys were aware that their parents' relationship was fractured, and they also knew their dad had been unhappy for many years. When the divorce was final, Jack's ex-wife returned to her native Philadelphia. Until his death, she would forever taunt him, refusing to let go. To this day, I am convinced that, in her mind, I never existed.

With his personal life in turmoil, Jack also had to deal with the numerous changes at the college which was compounded by the impact of the Vietnam War. Recruitment of male students and minority students continued to grow, partially because young men wanted to avoid the draft.

One spring, much to my horror, the black students held Jack hostage overnight in the library. Their demands were few, but had a significant impact on the college's budget. They requested an increase in library volumes that reflected Black history, an increase in black faculty, and the addition of a black counselor on the administration. After hours of deliberations and negotiations, and no sleep, the students freed Jack the next morning.

I didn't know anything about it until I arrived at my office after his release. It was a frightening experience not only for Jack, but also for the entire administration, because everyone wondered what was going to happen next. It was not a good time to be a college administrator.

Meanwhile, under Jack's tutelage I had become a successful admissions director. As my mentor, he was not only a dear friend, but a powerful role model. Lunch at nearby Noah's Ark Restaurant became more frequent. Over our favorite lunch—toasted Reuben sandwiches heaped with corn beef and sauerkraut—we discussed our work, our families, and our dreams. I became increasingly aware of his interest in me.

Many a morning, Jack appeared at my office door, his eyes sparkling. "Good Morning, Nancy," he'd say, or "How many applications did we get yesterday?" I came to look forward to these brief encounters, while my secretary, Claudia, smiled knowingly.

Being single for the first time in our adult lives, Jack and I quietly began to seek solace in each other's company. Never before had someone believed in my abilities, and that belief gave me a self-confidence that had been lacking in my life until then. Puzzled by the depth of my feelings, I simply did not know how to be anything except grateful for his friendship. While I was flattered by the attention, I felt that a deeper relationship had catastrophe written all over it. Our backgrounds and life experiences were very different. In addition, there was a significant disparity in our ages; he was fifty-two and I was thirty-six.

Jack was determined to move things along, while I tried to keep our relationship on a professional level. Following a national conference we both attended, I felt an intensity between us that flamed my heart. I was ignited in his presence, whether alone or in the company of others. We could no longer keep our distance. Like planets colliding in space, our passion exceeded all expectations. I would never be the same, nor would he. There was no turning back.

While privately, we were in ecstasy, the next two years were tumultuous. There was his former wife's mental health; his youngest son's drug problem; my son's unhappiness over his parents' divorce; Jack's jealousy of my friendship with other men; my envy of the new dean of students, who flirted with Jack; the college with all its challenges; and, finally, Jack's unexpected health problems.

We quietly and discreetly stole time together at my home in southwest St. Louis County. Jack often brought a bottle of French wine; some evenings I cooked, and other times we cooked together. We not only enjoyed sharing food and wine, but we also savored every word of our nonstop conversation. I was starved for someone who would listen without passing judgment, and he was starved for love. We talked about our families and friends, world events, politics, Broadway plays, music, books, and other subjects important to us. While these evenings sometimes were difficult for Bill, we did our best to make him feel part of our conversations.

As time went on and our relationship became public knowledge, we occasionally went to the University Club for dinner, or to a St. Louis Symphony Orchestra concert. Holding hands and scribbling notes on the program, we listened to the swelling crescendos of Dvorak's Symphony No. 9, or the works of Bach, Mozart, Beethoven, Bartok, and Sibelius. We loved them all.

With our busy schedules, Jack's children wanting time with their dad, and my need to be with my son, we often conveyed our feelings by phone or the written word. Jack loved words and wrote to me on whatever was available–hotel stationery, sheets from yellow legal pads, restaurant place mats, and even concert programs. Sometimes it was just a short note from his memo pad, "I love you more today than yesterday." "A lifetime would be too short." "The curves of your throat, the black of your hair, the dance of your eyes–just to know you are here." Or simply, "Hi, you missed a luncheon date with an interesting guy." Sometimes there would be a card from a fictitious person, signed James Blandford, or he would pen a quote from Alfred Lord Tennyson, Lord Byron, or this one by Milton Kaplan:

> "...I start up listening, listening as the window rattles
> And the floor crackles louder and louder
> Until suddenly the flame of your absence
> Blazes up and rages through my midnight mind."

Other times when we were miles apart, there would be long epistles:

Darling Nancy -

I have just returned to a very dark and almost depressing cabin. The drive back was spectacular. You weren't aware of it, but I stood and waited until they pushed your plane away. Maybe I was hoping they would de-plane you!

The past four days were incredibly happy ones for me. You are a great woman with an uncanny ability to make a man feel loved. Warm, perceptive, sensitive, responsive, observant, considerate–if anything happens to me, for God's sake hold yourself high for a man who deserves you.

You know what pressure is on me. I can't guess, let alone know, what the future holds. The dilemmas facing me are mine alone. No man - no woman, can pass on to another his or her moral responsibilities and ethical puzzles. Life puts on our backs the tests, the rocks, the timbers, and watches as we stagger. But fairly, life cheers and applauds when we carry the rock, pass the test, and handle the heavy timber.

The whole message I have for you is that for some reason, some mysterious human chemistry, I came in the past four days to see the woman that is in you. You can be proud of your ability to make a man taller.

This year can you create a new and broader system for telling the Lindenwood story to the students who must come if we are to survive, when what you want is to feel my hand?

Can you staff and train an admissions program, developing your own professionalism when what you want is to help me heal old and deep wounds that I have hidden from everyone but you?

Can you go to friends for dinner and find a partner has been subtly provided for you, and not respond to flattery, to good conversation, to the possibility of some fun, when what you want is not available?

Can you stand by and see me fighting for honor, for decency, for the respect of my sons and daughter, for my own self-respect, when what you want is to help, to share, and to strengthen our love?

Can you go home day after day alone?

Nancy, if we do what we must we will be better persons as a result–stronger, deeper, more human. I can feel your warm and gentle hand in mine.

Goodnight, Nancy,

Your Jack"

His words were like food for my soul. When his letters were few and far between I would reread every word—over and over again.

The winter and spring of 1973 were such a period, fraught with turbulence regarding the governance of the colleges. (By this time, there were two colleges: Lindenwood College for women and Lindenwood II, the men's college.)

In light of a financial deficit, the board of trustees had issued a directive:

> *...We have therefore ordered the administration to realign the operations of the colleges to reduce expenditures and to increase income in order to balance the operating budget by the 1974-1975 fiscal year.*

Jack, his chief officers, and various faculty leaders implemented a plan for merging and/or eliminating curricula that were not attracting sufficient enrollment. The plan recommended that academic departments be reduced from eighteen to eleven, and that several full-time faculty positions be eliminated.

A group of nine professors rose in opposition. Declaring a crisis of confidence in the leadership of Lindenwood, they distributed a twenty-three-page white paper, requesting shared governance and the search for a new president. Before the board or president could respond, the contents of the white paper were headlines in the St. Louis Post-Dispatch.

The internal struggle had become a story for the media to dissect. Baring Lindenwood's financial problems to the world, the white paper was devastating for Jack and for the campus community. I was absolutely crushed, and so were most of the faculty and staff. Except for the few dissidents—the authors of the white paper—Jack had been truly loved by a majority of his colleagues. We cried together in anguish over what this crisis meant for Jack's presidency and, ultimately, what it meant for my position.

By that time, our relationship had become a topic of campus conversation. Not only were we concerned about our future with The Lindenwood Colleges, but we feared the impact of the situation upon our special and treasured relationship.

But, at that moment, we need not have worried. The trustees issued a statement to the faculty:

> *...We have no inclination to accept the request made by a group of faculty members that we should seek a new president for the colleges.*

Although Jack's confidence was lifted, as the school year drew to a close, his days were consumed with debate and discussion surrounding the reduction of operating expenditures.

The last week of the academic year, his energy dwindled, and he developed shortness of breath and chest pain. Early one morning, he called me from the local hospital where he had been admitted for tests, and received his first diagnosis of cardiomyopathy. No visitors except Jack's children, the dean, and I were allowed to visit him. The goal was to keep tension and college issues at bay.

For the next three days, I spent my lunch hour with Jack at the hospital. We talked of many things: his prognosis, our plans for the summer, and when we were going to be married. He had already proposed and I had accepted. It was only a matter of when and where. We also contemplated our professional future–his as president and mine as admissions director.

Many good things happened at Lindenwood under Jack's leadership. He brought a new vision for academic reform, a new 4-1-4 calendar, with students spending January abroad before it was popular to do so, a new senior capstone course, a new fine arts center and riding stables; with the increase in male students, a separate college, Lindenwood II, was created.

Through his work with the Missouri independent colleges, a living memorial had been established that would allow every student in the state an opportunity to attend college. William H. Danforth, chancellor of Washington University, wrote after Jack's death, "Jack is responsible, more than any other single human being for the state scholarship program in the State of Missouri."

Without a doubt, Jack and I made a great team, and we looked forward to our continued work at Lindenwood, but there were many unanswered questions. Would the board of trustees allow me to continue in my position, or would I need to assume the traditional role of president's wife and official campus hostess? While it was not acceptable at that time in history for a college president's wife to work, I believed I was capable of performing the duties required in both roles.

After three days in the hospital, Jack was dismissed with strict orders to take life easy for the next three months. Spending the summer at Jack's Maine cabin seemed like a logical thing to do. By then, I loved him from the depths of my soul and wanted to spend whatever time we had together. Unwavering in our commitment, we determined nothing was going to keep us apart.

As the ambulance sped toward Port Columbus, I looked at my sleeping husband, barely able to see his face in the darkness. I silently thanked God for bringing us together and for the love Jack had showered on me. And then, suddenly, we arrived at the airport and I was jolted back to reality.

The flight to St. Louis and the frightening ambulance ride to the hospital is a nightmare in my memory cells. Not only did Jack have oxygen on the plane, but he took a Valium and two more Lasix to keep his lungs from filling up with fluid. I wondered how much Lasix one could take. Seven in a day seemed excessive to me. The hour-long flight seemed forever, and is a blur in my mind.

Arriving at our destination, we were greeted by two paramedics. I was so grateful they were there. They immediately checked Jack's heart and pulse rate, lifted him on to the gurney, covered him with a blanket, and raced through the long corridors to the waiting ambulance. I didn't think I would be able to keep pace. The noise in the crowded airport sounded like bees buzzing in their hive. Speakers blared, babies cried, and people talked and laughed. There were throngs of humanity everywhere as we pushed our way through what seemed like a long, dark tunnel.

Jogging for miles, or so it seemed, I suffered from shortness of breath by the time I flung myself into the back of the ambulance. The siren screeched as we raced over the treacherous, snow-packed streets to St. Luke's Hospital. The shrill sound of the siren made me even more fearful. Jack's breathing was increasingly labored. One of the medics monitored him every second, while I wiped the beads of perspiration from his forehead. Would we make it in time? I wondered if Jack could possibly survive such a hair-raising trip.

Arriving at St. Luke's, we bypassed the emergency room and went directly to 2600–the cardiac intensive care unit on the second floor. I didn't even fill out the routine admission documents until the next day.

A sense of peace and comfort came over me, like reaching a safe haven after difficult travels. I was so relieved to see Sylvia Henderson, the leader of the ICU nurses team on the three-to-eleven shift. It was after eleven o'clock, but she was still on duty, awaiting Jack's arrival. Sylvia had been Jack's nurse on our previous visit. A beautiful woman with dancing blue eyes, a creamy, smooth complexion, and short-cropped light brown hair streaked with blonde, like rays of sunlight, Sylvia was probably in her early thirties. We would become close friends in the weeks ahead.

Dr. Rainey finally arrived around two o'clock in the morning. I vividly recall his saying to Sylvia and me, "The visitor rule does not apply to Mrs. Brown. Nancy, I do not want you to leave the hospital. The nurses will give you a place to keep your clothes in their locker room along with a pillow and blanket." I was exhausted and didn't care if I slept or where I slept, just so I could be with Jack.

On this, the longest night of my life, I held Jack's hand while his restless body tried to relax. Touching was an important part of our relationship, so we communicated with our fingertips. As I recall, I sat in the dark with only the light from the nurse's station for illumination. Occasionally, I would hear physicians being paged over the hospital intercom.

For hours, white-coated doctors and nurses came and went every few minutes. The nurses moved quietly, like paper angels, and occasionally their rubber-soled shoes squeaked on the terrazzo floors. I was mesmerized by the waves on the heart monitor.

With Jack in good hands, sometime between three and four o'clock, I fell into an exhausted sleep on a worn, brown vinyl sofa in the ICU waiting room. Situated immediately around the corner from cardiac intensive care, and back to back with Jack's room, the waiting room was spacious with several couches, end tables and lamps, and a television set. Two tall windows looked out over a courtyard leading to St. Luke's School of Nursing. The walls were a depressing shade of greenish-beige. That night, I was relieved to have the room to myself. It would soon become my home.

A St. Louis native, I had been treated at St. Luke's emergency room as a child, my son was born there, and in 1974, I was a consultant to the radiology department. In addition, Jack had been a patient on two occasions. Having a history with the place, I felt at home, although this time it was a worried and uneasy comfort. It was more like being lost in a small boat on the open sea, not knowing in which direction I was headed.

Chapter III

LIFE IN SUSPENSION

"When the expected course of everyday life is interrupted, we realize we are like shipwrecked people trying to keep their balance on a miserable plank in the open sea, having forgotten where they came from and not knowing whither they are drifting."

—*Albert Einstein*

Day 2

From the light of dawn, the first day was unnerving. Awakening after three hours of sleep, I heard the hushed voices of student nurses on their way to breakfast. As I rolled off the cold, clammy sofa and rushed to Jack's room, I felt like a disheveled street person, having slept in yesterday's clothes.

Everything looked different in the morning light. A sterile, antiseptic, and pungent-smelling environment, the cardiac ICU unit was a circular space with ten individual cubicles surrounding the nurses' station.

I smiled and said, "Good morning, Jack." He glared at me, his eyes transmitting fear and apprehension. In a demanding, gravely voice, he asked, "Where in the hell have you been?"

I had been at his every beck and call for months. Was he trying to make me feel guilty for catching a little shuteye? I couldn't believe it. While those were my immediate thoughts, I knew deep in my soul that my hero had fallen. Now, he needed me to boost his spirits. In response to his question, I quietly replied, "Sleeping on the waiting room sofa." He looked at me in disbelief.

Thank heavens, at that moment Sylvia appeared to tell Jack about the tests he would have later in the morning. Sylvia would become his favorite nurse, and mine, as well. She had a wonderful way of making a patient feel safe and comfortable, but on that first morning, Jack was so frightened there was nothing she, or anyone, could do or say to make him feel better. He was like a child in the dark, fearful of the bogey man hiding under the bed.

A natural-born worrier, Jack lay in his hospital bed and fretted about the college. The budget had to be trimmed, and perhaps a few of the faculty would be asked to leave. This scenario was reminiscent of our last days at Lindenwood. He also worried about his children, particularly his oldest son, Anthony, who was in the process of divorce, and David, whom we hoped had finally given up drugs. Jack was also apprehensive about Bill, with whom we had left the full responsibility for the president's house, our recently completed retreat cottage, and a pregnant Arabian mare.

No matter what I said to try to ease Jack's anguish, I was unable to remove the torment going on in his brain. His anxiety level was great, and, having nothing else to do, he tortured himself with things he could do nothing about. Hanging out there, like dangling participles, were numerous undone tasks which I would somehow have to see to completion, or delegate to someone else.

Jack's greatest disappointment was not being able to complete the final accreditation report for St. Lawrence University. The report to the Middle States Association was due. Some editing had been accomplished, but it was obvious that Lewis Cary, the assistant who had accompanied Jack on the trip, would have to complete and submit the final review of St. Lawrence.

A graduate of Gettysburg College, Lewis was bright and astute, and his demeanor was always calm and controlled. Jack had a great deal of respect for his professionalism. Nonetheless, Jack was frustrated that he wouldn't be able to complete the project for his dear friend and president of St. Lawrence, Frank Piskor.

After Jack's death, Dr. Piskor wrote me a letter that epitomized the impact Jack had on the St. Lawrence faculty:

> "Many, many people at St. Lawrence University had you on their minds and hearts yesterday. As you probably know, Jack was a longtime, personal friend dating back to his Temple University days; but on his several visits here he stimulated so many that the news of his death made a tremendous impact.
>
> Your husband was kind, friendly, intellectually honest, and an unusually provocative colleague. I shall treasure our most recent private conversations about my college, about values in the contemporary society, and the compelling need to get away from the valuelessness that plagues all of us. What a book he planned to write in the values area!
>
> It is our institutional loss that we shall not have the benefit of his wisdom in a written document, but I shall always treasure

my notes of his verbal report because he was insightful, full of
wisdom, critical, and supportive."

With one project out of the way, my thoughts turned to
Jack's latest newspaper column, "As an Educator Sees It," already
overdue at *The Daily Jeffersonian* in Cambridge, Ohio. Between
whiffs on the portable oxygen tank, Jack had dictated a rough
draft the previous Saturday. Much to his consternation, the copy
would be late. As his editor, I needed to massage the text, make
changes, and mail a clean copy as soon as possible. My load would
have been lighter had computers given birth to laptops before
1978.

But my first priority was Jack. The task would have to wait
until the next day, or whenever. Jack fussed all day about what I
needed to do. Sick as he was, he gave marching orders to me and
some of the medical staff, almost as if he were a general directing
a campaign.

I spent that first morning at the hospital with Jack and
a medical student whose name was Michael. With Jack in a
wheelchair, we traversed the halls of the hospital from radiology
to the catheterization lab to urology. After numerous x-rays, Dr.
Hal Sumner, chief of radiology, informed us that Jack's doctors
wanted to rule out the possibility of blood clots.

A long-time friend of mine, Dr. Sumner had an engaging
personality, overflowing with warmth and caring. Short in stature,
with an egg-shaped, balding head, he wore black horn-rimmed
glasses. There was something about the way he moved that
reminded me of a scampering chipmunk, flitting here and there.

I had first met Dr. Sumner following my graduation from
college when I worked as a medical librarian for Washington
University Medical School's radiology department. Years later,
it was Dr. Sumner who hired me to help reorganize outpatient
procedures for various radiological examinations at St. Luke's
Hospital.

After I moved to Ohio, I never expected to see him again.
What a welcome sight his face was that morning! I felt blessed
and secure, surrounded by friends who were taking care of my
husband.

Because of Jack's fear of blood clots, our conversation with
Dr. Sumner was unsettling. As the day wore on, any comments or
explanations from nurses or doctors set off the electrical impulses

in Jack's nervous system. Looking into his glassy eyes, you could almost see the impulses rippling through his body. Even if the conversation was positive, Jack took the negative, role-playing the devil's advocate, a favorite ploy of his during faculty meetings. He didn't want to believe what the doctors were telling him. Grimacing, I gritted my teeth, tried my best to face reality, and listened carefully to what the doctors had to say.

After more than two hours of examinations, Jack was exhausted. Returning to the ICU, he sighed with relief as he crawled in bed. Dodging the tubes and pushing the oxygen mask aside, I planted a big kiss on his lips. As he closed his eyes, I quietly escaped to freshen up and grab a quick lunch in the hospital coffee shop. Whatever had happened to breakfast?

Still dressed in yesterday's clothes and feeling like an unmade bed, I stopped in the nurses' locker room to wash my face and brush my teeth. Looking into a most unflattering mirror, I said a silent prayer, blessing whoever invented make-up. As if I had suddenly become a fish, my eyes were bloodshot and surrounded by puffy mountains of dry, scaly skin. Hastily covering the dark circles and other unsightly blemishes, I applied my favorite crimson lipstick. I thought how refreshing a hot shower might feel, but none was to be seen. My body was so tired with little sleep and no food. Except for water, coffee, or a diet Coke, I had not eaten since the previous evening on the airplane.

I changed into black slacks, my favorite red turtleneck sweater, and the same brown penny loafers I'd been wearing. Red always had been my best color, but it didn't do much for my looks on that day. I dragged myself to the elevator and down to the crowded coffee shop. I found a spare stool at the counter.

Dressed in a pink and white striped jumper, the petite waitress was an attractive brunette with a beautiful smile. Her name was Cindy. She was friendly, inquiring where I was from, but I was too tired to talk. I requested a grilled cheese sandwich, my comfort food, and a Coke. The order came with French fries and coleslaw, so I was sufficiently nourished. I wanted a cup of coffee to keep me awake, but I was to meet my parents in the waiting room at one-thirty and it was already one-fifteen.

I had called my mother and dad the previous evening and they were, of course, shocked to learn Jack was in the hospital again, and that we were in St. Louis. Feeling rejuvenated after lunch, I hurried to check on Jack before meeting my parents. His eyes were closed and the nurse had turned off the overhead light, leaving the door slightly ajar. I retraced my steps and headed for the waiting room.

Having lost his hair thirty years earlier, and looking not a day over sixty, my dad always appeared the same to me. Raised on a cattle farm in Mississippi, Daddy was a southern gentleman, a devout Christian, and a proud Goldwater Republican. A quiet man, he was devastated by the suicide of my grandfather and, then later, the tragic death of my eleven-year-old brother. (I didn't know my grandfather had shot himself until after my father's death.) He seldom, if ever, spoke of my brother.

While expressing his feelings did not come easily, he loved my mother dearly, and I knew he loved me, too. As I grew up and became a young woman, he would often say "What ever happened to the little girl who used to sit on my lap?" He wanted me always to be his little girl.

Linwood and Esther Neblett Alvis on their fiftieth wedding anniversary.

My mother was one of five children, two boys and three girls. The siblings were scattered across the country, but they and their families were an important part of my childhood, as was my father's family. Daddy had one sister, three brothers, and two half-brothers. While I had a lot of my mother's personality traits, I looked more like my father, with his dark skin and brown eyes.

A fabulous cook who loved to entertain, my mother was also the queen of volunteers. Active and energetic at the age of sixty-eight, she was president of the St. Louis Salvation Army Women's Auxiliary, and one of the pillars of her church, located just a few blocks from the hospital.

Married during the Depression, and products of a long family lineage of educated and hard-working people, my parents learned what values were important to success. Those values of honesty, integrity, faith in God, discipline, and hard work were instilled in me at a very early age and, I believe, gave me the necessary tools to survive any catastrophe. Daddy was highly disciplined and organized, and wasn't too happy if the rest of his family didn't follow suit.

From the earliest I can remember, I was expected to get up in the morning when awakened. If I did not, the pillow was pulled out from under my head. According to Daddy, pillows were bad for your health; I could become a hunchback.

As children, my brother and I were expected to go to Sunday school and church every Sunday of the year, whatever the weather and however we felt. After church, the Sabbath was a day of rest. We were not allowed to go to the movies or birthday parties on Sunday. When I had to tell that to my friends, I was not a happy camper. Birthday parties were a big void in my life. Though I didn't always like going to church every Sunday, and would later rebel, my strong faith and spiritual values carried me through numerous shattering events in my life.

My father's mother–Mother Alvis we called her–was a very important role model for me. When I was five years old, my Grandfather Neblett (my mother's father) died and Mother Alvis came to St. Louis to take care of me while my parents traveled to Tennessee for the funeral. I remember sitting on my bed watching Mother Alvis as she combed the long, silky black hair that cascaded down her back. She told me there was Indian blood in our family. She certainly looked as if there might be. A hardworking farm woman, her features were striking, with high cheek bones and dark brown, almost black, eyes. She kept herself trim and stood erect at all times.

Until she died at the age of ninety, Mother Alvis exercised daily in front of an open window, whether it was winter, spring, summer, or fall. Before the breathing exercises, deep knee bends, and toe touches, she drank eight glasses of water. She said it kept her blood clean.

Although Mother Alvis raised four sons, one daughter, and two stepsons, from the time her husband died when she was fifty, she lived alone another forty years. She was a strong-willed, independent woman for whom I had great respect. I loved her dearly, though I did not see her nearly enough.

I have often thought of my grandmother and wondered how she survived on her own all those years. Jesus went to the desert for forty days and forty nights to ask God what he should do. My grandmother lived alone for forty years, deliberately and without regret, carving out her own identity as a woman. Her characteristics of strength and independence had been passed on to me, but did I have the same survival instincts?

My most important role model, my mother, could have been Mother Alvis's daughter. The middle child of five and also the middle of three girls, she defied the notion that the middle child has a difficult row to hoe. Her mother had died of tuberculosis, and when Mother was twelve, her father remarried. She took her eight-year-old sister, Nancy, under her wing. My mother would forever be a role model for my Aunt Nancy and her two children, Doug and Connie, as well as for me.

From the time we moved from St. Louis to Mexico, Missouri when I was ten, Daddy was a manufacturer's representative, traveling five days a week. He left home Monday morning before I went to school, and returned Friday in time for supper. Because that left my mother without a car, she walked, or rode the bus. I biked across town to junior high school, and when my brother, seven years younger, entered first grade, he walked three blocks to school. One Friday when my father was returning home, he was so busy listening to the car radio that he drove right past my mother, who was walking home. That was the last car Daddy purchased with a radio.

There were certain advantages to my dad's absence during the week. Although I still had my chores, life with my mother was more flexible. We had fun, and I learned many things from my mother, including a love for reading, cooking, and entertaining. She also taught me to play bridge, to sew on an old Singer treadle machine, and to knit. Knitting was her passion, and I have a closet filled with her knitted coats and sweaters.

My mother did her own cleaning, except when we were going to have company. She did everything–window washing, painting, weeding, and mowing the grass. My mother was also good with a hammer. By the time my father returned on Friday, the house and yard were in order, and my mother could rest for the weekend, but she rarely did. As I got older, I also did my share of the housework; ironing was my least favorite chore, and still is.

Seldom taking time for herself, my mother was always doing for others–a neighbor, a needy family, or for a church dinner or bake sale. Every week, she baked several loaves of bread, giving two away and keeping one for us. When she got older, she continued her giving nature by serving Meals-on-Wheels. I admired my mother's generosity, her caring nature, her faith in God, her dedication to her family, and her strength to carry on in my father's absence. There were times, I know, when she was lonely, particularly after my brother died, and I went to college. Her strong faith enabled her to move on. What a wonderful legacy my mother left me.

Those family roots gave me the stamina, the courage, and the spiritual tools to support my husband through the long days and nights in the ICU. Hiding my fears, I was there for Jack. My strong faith was my rudder and, like Mother Alvis, I stood tall, surviving whatever came my way, with grace and dignity.

But on that day, as I greeted my parents, I no doubt looked exhausted, in spite of my attempt to look spiffy in my red sweater. My mother, dressed in navy slacks and a light blue sweater, had tears in her eyes. Daddy was his usual sober self in a gray flannel golf cap and his maroon plaid leisure jacket, my gift many Christmases before. As I looked at him, I wondered if he'd ever give that tacky jacket away. Since moving to Ohio, I'd seen my parents several times a year, and my dad invariably wore his maroon plaid jacket.

Jack was too ill for visitors; nevertheless, from that first day on, my parents plowed through the snow almost every afternoon to be with me. Without their daily visits, I might have looked like a bag lady, for my mother laundered or dry-cleaned my clothes each week. My mother's favorite motto was: when traveling you should take half as many clothes as you think you need and twice the amount of money. I had adopted her slogan, and thus, I had left home with only a few clothes.

Some days my parents arrived to find me in less than a talkative mood. Staring at the unsightly beige wall or closing my eyes, I would pretend to nap. They would watch television or talk with other visitors about the ever-continuing snow storm ravaging the Midwest. Grateful for their company, I shudder to think what my existence might have been without their visits. I was so consumed with Jack's critical situation, that without daily, stimulating conversation with my parents, I just might have gone out of my mind. Some days I felt like my brain cells were slowly being engulfed by a dense fog.

On that first day, after hugs and kisses, we sat down on the uncomfortable sofa where I had slept in the early morning hours. While I was apprehensive about being away from Jack, I knew one of the nurses would come if he needed me. My body was physically tired and emotionally overwrought, but I forced myself to talk about Jack's precarious condition.

My parents were concerned about my living in the hospital, and also wondered if they should go to Ohio to be with Bill. Fortunately, I was able to convince them that Bill would be fine, and that David and Katie were nearby if he needed them. At seventeen, Bill's confidence would have been shaken if his grandparents had suddenly appeared on the doorstep. He would think we didn't trust him. Besides, I did not think my parents should drive to Ohio with the treacherous condition of the roads, and flying was not their preferred mode of travel.

As for my sleeping at their apartment, there was no way I was going to leave Jack until he improved significantly. My parents understood, but were still worried. This wasn't a new thing.

Since the day I was born, my mother had worried about me. Often, Daddy would chuckle and say, "Nancy, you don't have to worry about anything because your mother will do all the worrying for you." And so, my philosophy always has been not to worry, and to think positively except, perhaps, for the situation in which I then found myself.

As my parents departed into the blowing snow that first afternoon, I ducked into the nearly empty coffee shop for a cup of java and a cigarette. During my teenage years, I'd begun smoking with my friends at slumber parties. My parents abhorred the nasty habit. My mother's favorite greeting after a slumber party was never, "Good morning," but rather, "You reek." Consequently, I avoided smoking in their presence. Reaching midlife, I never smoked more than ten cigarettes a day, but even that was too many. Since Jack smoked a pipe only on special occasions, I was smoking less and less, and never at public functions.

Putting out my cigarette, I returned to the ICU to find Jack in a great deal of discomfort; breathing was labored and he was perspiring profusely. I was frightened and clutched his hand for assurance. In only moments, Dr. Rainey appeared. Jack had developed tachycardia–an extremely rapid ventricular heartbeat. Not sure electric shock would be successful, Dr. Rainey prescribed Digitalis. Over the next half-hour, the heart rate slowly decreased and tensions subsided. Dr. Rainey quietly asked me to join him in the waiting room.

"Jack is a very sick man," he said. "I must ask you to help

keep him as calm as possible." Without a biopsy, there was no way to know the extent of heart muscle damage, and Jack was far too ill for such a procedure. "Under no circumstances, do I want Jack's children to visit him," Dr. Rainey continued. "The emotion of such an encounter could push his life over the edge."

How in the world was I going to relay this message to David, Philip, Anthony, and Barbara? Jack's children were all young adults, struggling with their families and their careers. I knew none of them could afford the trip to St. Louis, and I certainly did not have the funds to purchase their airplane tickets. I also knew if they could find a way, they would rush to their father's side. They loved him with a passion, and the feeling was mutual.

At the time, I felt the doctor's decision was right and I had to live with it. Would his final days have been more or less stressful had his children been there? Perhaps, he would not have suffered as long. Would I have handled it differently today? My instinctive reaction was to do everything in my power to assure Jack's survival. The doctors never uttered the words death or dying. Had the doctors told me Jack was going to die, I would have made sure his kids were at his side. In the absence of real knowledge, I refused to give up hope. Deep in my soul, there will remain forever a pang of guilt that his children were not given the opportunity to say goodbye. But, for that matter, I didn't say goodbye, either.

Needing to mull over my conversation with Dr. Rainey, when evening came I dragged myself back to the hospital coffee shop for dinner. The food did not look appetizing, or taste good. I certainly needed the strength, but I was not hungry for nourishment of my body. I needed strength for my soul. I wondered where the hospital chapel was located.

Nibbling on a dry, flavorless hamburger and uninteresting tossed salad with its tasteless tomatoes, I contemplated the best way to relay the doctor's orders to David and his siblings. How was I to be diplomatic, as well as caring, without provoking their wrath? I needed their emotional support. How in the hell was I to handle all the crises alone? Though my parents were supportive, they were not Jack's blood family. I needed David to be there. What a dilemma. I knew God would be my co-pilot, showing me the way.

Talking to myself, planning the best approach with my stepchildren, I let my bleary gaze roam around the brightly lit room. It was long past the dinner hour, and I was virtually alone, except for two waitresses dressed in their matching pink-striped shirtwaists and white aprons. The room was comfortable and inviting, with square tables and seats for four, as well as booths along the window, and the counter seats where I had lunched.

The cheerful decor was restful with its green and pink floral wallpaper and scenic prints nicely framed and hung on two sides of the room. The opposite walls were solid glass, looking out over the lobby and a drugstore just off the main entrance. As the days went by, I would become a regular customer; the coffee shop became my favorite hangout, like Kizers Drugstore, when I was a teenager.

Until recently, hospitals were designed only for patients, not families. Other than "my room," the coffee shop was the only place to relax, and the food was certainly an improvement over the hospital cafeteria. The latter was mainly for employees, but I was offered a pass and did eat there on several occasions. However, I preferred the quiet surroundings of the coffee shop.

Seated in a window booth, I could watch the world go by as the winter storm continued, read a book, write in my journal, or jot notes to my family.

Having finished my dinner, I hurried back to the ICU. Jack was dozing. In a constant state of fear, I checked to be sure the heart monitor was still functioning. The condensation in the oxygen mask told me his lungs were still working. Wiping his perspiring brow, I whispered I was going down the hall to find a phone booth to call Lewis Cary, David, and Bill. Jack nodded, never opening his weary eyes.

My first call was to Lewis. Expressing great concern for Jack, Lewis was more than willing to prepare the final accreditation report. What a relief. I also placed a call to Rupert Henderson, academic dean of the college, who had been at the Manse the previous afternoon. It was unbelievable to me that we had left home only twenty-four hours before.

In terms of administrative style, Rupert was Jack's opposite. A former Presbyterian minister, he was laid back and seldom, if ever, flustered. Of medium height with a full head of curly salt-and-pepper hair, Rupert stood erect at all times, with his suit coat buttoned, as if he were an Army sergeant giving orders.

I had nothing definitive to report, but Rupert had been anxiously awaiting news of Jack. He seemed overjoyed to hear from me, and sent best wishes from many of the faculty and staff.

I conveyed Jack's trust in him to carry on in his absence.

Leaving Jack to make these calls would become increasingly difficult in the days ahead. When I attempted to leave, even to go to the bathroom, he'd be frightened. Where was I going and when would I return?

Today's wireless telephone might have been helpful in the waiting room, but I would have been too guarded to carry on a meaningful conversation in Jack's presence. The only solution was to quietly slip out when he was sleeping. The phone booth and the coffee shop were the only escape from the smell of sickness and the gloom which hung like a dense fog over the ICU. Though I was surrounded by nurses, doctors, medical students, and visitors, never had I felt so alone.

Perhaps, there was one other time.

When my brother, William, died unexpectedly, suddenly our home was filled with aunts, uncles, and cousins. Giving up my room to relatives was like being left out in sub-zero weather with no parka for protection. Michael, my friend and former boyfriend, came to be with me. Sitting on the back steps, we cried and talked until long after dark. Although we had dated throughout our sophomore and junior years in high school, we had parted ways the previous summer. Much to my chagrin, he had a new girlfriend. Nonetheless, I put my head on Michael's shoulder, he held my hand, warmed my soul, and soothed my tears–tears that felt as large as hail stones. Lonely at seventeen, I had a friend.

At the funeral and graveside service, I didn't hear a word the minister said. Sitting under a blue tent next to my composed father, I stared in disbelief at the hole in the ground where my brother's casket lay. Angry at William for dying, I sobbed long after everyone had departed the grave site.

When my parents realized I wasn't in the limousine, our minister, Rufus Gary, returned to get me. A tall, burly Dutchman who looked like a linebacker, he gently put his arm around me as we made our way to the car. Surrounded by friends and relatives, all I could think about was the fact that I now was an only child, alone and desolate.

Thinking about those long-ago days did not help me escape my loneliness. I returned my thoughts to the present and the phone calls I needed to make. Calling Bill, David, and Katie was painful, on both ends of the line.

Reaching out to them with five hundred miles in between, they seemed light years away. Oh, I needed their warmth and caring touch. Captain of the ship for the indefinite future, Bill was managing all the pets and phone calls.

In good spirits, he talked about basketball practice, games, and his friends at John Glenn High School. A new driver with his own 1969 red, Ford pick-up truck, Bill plowed six miles through the snow each evening to our cottage. He was proud of his truck, purchased with his own money the previous summer. He said the snow drifts were six feet high in some places, and that driving was akin to skiing through a spiraling tunnel.

Echo, our twelve-year-old Arabian mare, always awaited his arrival. Named after our favorite lake in Maine, she was in foal and scheduled to give birth in June of that year. She spent those cold winter days in the small barn piled with bales of hay. Bill fed her grain purchased at the local feed store; he used a shovel to break the ice in the water trough.

After a tearful conversation, I assured Bill everything was going to be all right, and that I would call him again soon. Ever so briefly, I placed the phone in its cradle, and then dialed David's number. As directly as I could, I spit out Dr. Rainey's words about no visitors. Accepting the news graciously, he understood his father's emotions only too well. To my pleasant surprise, he offered to share the doctor's comments with his brothers and sister. What a burden lifted!

Phone calls in the small, narrow booth, with its bright light and tiny oscillating fan, were exhausting. It felt like I was having a hot flash in a broom closet. Four phone calls drained all the strength I had for that evening.

In the days ahead, I talked for hours in the warm, stuffy phone booth. Those conversations, with family and friends, were my lifeline to the world. I sifted the news carefully, sharing only the good messages with Jack. Normally an open person and wearing my emotions on my sleeve, I found it nearly unbearable to have to hide my thoughts and feelings. My relationship with Jack was based on honest and open communication. To suddenly avoid sharing important news or information tied my stomach in knots, but I zipped my lip.

Making sure Jack was asleep on that particular evening, I returned to "my room." The television was broadcasting the latest news: Senator Hubert Humphrey had died and the networks were showing a special about his funeral. With the reality of what I might face, I could not bear to watch. Turning off the television, I left the room to wander. It was late, almost eleven o'clock. My attention was drawn to the window as mountains of snow fell into the courtyard below. I wondered how it would feel to go skiing off the hospital roof.

Later, I paced the long corridor with its attractive tan and gold vertical-striped wallpaper. Located between the ICU waiting room and the elevators, there were two tastefully decorated alcoves on either side of the hallway. Several Chippendale-style love seats covered in blue-green damask were flanked by cherry wood end tables. Tall, graceful brass lamps with charcoal gray shades graced the tables, giving a calm, subdued look to the room. With not another human being visible, the atmosphere radiated an aura of peace and tranquility. Hungry for the serenity, I discarded my loafers and curled up on one of the love seats.

I closed my eyes as my uneasy brain jumped around in search of some focus. Life, as I knew it, hung in the balance, with my world turned upside down and inside out. As Albert Einstein had said,

> "When the expected course of everyday life is interrupted, we realize we are like shipwrecked people trying to keep their balance on a miserable plank in the open sea, having forgotten where they came from and not knowing whither they are drifting."

Where was I? It felt like Disney World's Space Mountain with its high peaks and deep valleys, running through the dark of night? It was the same gut-wrenching feeling–as if I had opened a door into a dark room turned topsy-turvy with no exit. What was I to do?

Having a positive attitude from the cradle, and believing in the philosophy of Dr. Norman Vincent Peale, I asked myself, "How do you have a positive attitude in a life-threatening situation?" Jack was so emotionally distraught. How in the world was I going to elevate his spirits? Above all, I would have to be calm and cheerful, with my thoughts collected.

How could I smile when I wanted to cry? Usually in control of my emotions, I simply did not know where I was going to draw the strength and the courage to hide my feelings. My faith in God had carried me through tough times before, and I prayed it would again.

Suddenly, approaching footsteps brought me back to reality. Carolyn, a tall, blond ICU nurse, came sprinting down the hall, quietly calling my name. Jack's heart rate had escalated into ventricular tachycardia again, followed by cardiac arrest. My spirits shriveled as I raced back to the ICU. Jack's bed was surrounded by five or six nurses and doctors, as well as the red crash car. There were so many bodies I could barely see Jack over the bobbing heads, and the hands darting here and there. I stood at the door, watching as they used electric paddles, trying to shock his heart into rhythm.

Finally, their heroic efforts brought him back to life, but the heart rate was still too fast. Long into the night, the small room was crowded with dedicated caregivers trying to save my husband's life: There was Dr. Ganga from India, chief cardiology resident; tall, thin Dr. Delhein, senior cardiac ICU staff doctor; Dr. Gannon, cardiology intern; and Sylvia, who kept me informed throughout the unsettling night. Poor Sylvia, with one crisis after another, she worked at least three hours overtime that night.

No one has ever explained to me why heart patients often develop serious problems in the late evening hours. The crash cart never rolled except at night, and new cardiac patients arrived most every evening. Cardiac nurses on the three-to-eleven shift worked long into the night, stabilizing their patients, and completing volumes of paper work. Hospital computers had not yet arrived on the scene. Each patient's ongoing history had to be written by hand, and detailed instructions on each person had to be completed for the next personnel shift.

For hours, in a daze, I paced back and forth between Jack's cubicle and my room. Shortly after one a.m., Dr. Rainey arrived, accompanied by Dr. Benjamin Poole, a pulmonary specialist. My first major decision arrived with them. Jack had developed pulmonary edema. A respirator or ventilator was necessary to clear the fluid from his lungs and help him breathe. There seemed to be no alternative.

I liked Dr. Poole instantly, and came to admire his intelligence, his perception, and his caring bedside manner. A handsome man, Dr. Poole was probably in his early forties, five-foot-ten inches tall with coal-black hair and piercing olive green eyes that radiated in the dimly lit room. He explained the process, and though the necessity was clear, I knew Jack would detest being confined by such a monstrous contraption. He was already breathing with the help of supplemental oxygen, and now his lungs would be assisted by artificial means. Days later, Jack would be extremely angry with me for approving the respirator.

Knowing now what I didn't know then, I might not have given my permission. Jack probably would not have lived another twenty-seven days, nor would he have endured the pain. Today, in the twenty-first century, he would have had a living will. The decision would have been his, not mine. What a relief for my conscience that would have been. At that moment, however, whatever it took for Jack to live was all I wanted.

With the arrival of the respirator came tubes and intravenous catheters that protruded from every conceivable orifice in my husband's body. Pumps were hissing, monitors were beeping, and bottles were dripping. Walking a tight rope between this world and the next, my husband's life hung in the balance. Ashen, he lay trapped in his own body, unable to talk, and no doubt silently screaming, "Get me out of here."

Suctioning of the phlegm stuck in his throat sent out raspy, haunting bellows. I was mesmerized by the pendulum of the heart monitor and the beep-beep of its sound, along with the gurgling of the respirator.

With all sense of time and perspective obliterated, the rhythm of my life had gone haywire. Unanswered questions tumbled through my mind like wet towels in the clothes dryer. What kind of nightmare was this? Although the world was swirling around me, I was an observer floating in some other place. This wasn't happening to me. Who was I and where was I going? Meaningless details of my life danced around in search of meaning. For the first time in my life, I was powerless.

Exhausted in the wee hours, I stretched out on my sofa. Broken-hearted and sobbing into the lumpy, mothball-smelling pillow, it didn't matter whether the tears cried into silk, flannel, or leather. Our first summer together was vivid in my mind, and the memories eased my pain.

*O*n June 14, 1973, John Anthony Brown and I were married at the Presbyterian Church in Kirkwood, Missouri, less than a mile from my home. I had been a member of the Gothic stone church for several years, and was fond of the minister, the Reverend Clint Keyes. On a sun-drenched June morning, Clint, with his gray hair and mustache, was dressed in a long white robe. His black horn-rimmed glasses framed his warm eyes. The vivid colors in the thirty-foot stained-glass windows reflected on our gold wedding bands that rested on Clint's open bible.

It was a small wedding, with only my parents, Bill, and four of our colleagues to witness our vows. Jack's eyes glistened as they danced, and he smiled from ear to ear. Distinguished looking in his light grey linen sport coat, a paisley blue tie, and pin-striped grey slacks, Jack looked the happiest I had ever seen him.

My yellow-and-white flowered chiffon dress, the color of daisies, floated gently around my body. The fabric was so light and airy I felt as if I had nothing on. The billowing sleeves barely touched my arms. I carried a dozen long-stemmed yellow roses.

I have a faint recollection of organ music soaring to the rafters and a voice singing "Ave Maria." What the organist played, what the soloist sang, and what the minister said I am unable to retrieve from my conscious mind. I was bursting with joy. It was like a dream. I could hardly believe Jack and I were husband and wife. Following a luncheon with family and friends, we drove to my home, packed our suitcases, and departed for Maine.

Thirteen-year-old Bill, dressed in a burgundy and white-striped seersucker sport coat and burgundy slacks, and with stringy bangs almost covering his eyes, looked sad and forlorn as our car backed out the driveway. Probably thinking he had lost his mother, Bill spent the summer with his father and his grandparents. Since the day of his birth, it was our longest separation.

After spending our wedding night at a hotel on the outskirts of St. Louis, Jack and I drove east across the flatlands of Illinois, into the rolling hills of Indiana and Ohio, along the southern perimeter of Lake Erie, and through the northwest corner of Pennsylvania. Since Jack was recuperating, I did a great deal of the driving. Radiant and overjoyed to be together, we talked our way across the country. Time was of no importance. While the trip could be made in two long days, we took a leisurely three-day drive.

Entering the flowing terrain of New York State, we passed through the Finger Lakes region, viewing miles and miles of grape vineyards. Turning northeastward, we traversed the mountains, the green valleys, and the charming hamlets in Vermont. It was my first time to Vermont, and the beauty was breathtaking. Once in New Hampshire, we visited Dartmouth College, nestled at the foot of the White Mountains in the village of Hanover. In the center of the campus green, there were magnificent red maple trees and prolific rose and lilac bushes, with park benches around the periphery.

Much to our surprise, we viewed hikers making their way over the Appalachian Trail. At the far end of the campus green, a stark white brick chapel with its tall spires was almost eclipsed by the majestic White Mountains rising in the distance. While our stop at Dartmouth was less than an hour, the site was one we would not forget. By mid afternoon, we were eager to move on, in order to reach our cabin before dark.

Arriving in Maine several hours later, all we could see for miles were tall pine trees reaching upward. Along the way, there were logging camps; timbers were placed in a nearby river to float downstream to the mills, where the wood pulp would be made into paper. The first whiff of the sulfurous fumes from the paper mill nauseated me, as if I were pregnant. Heaven forbid.

I vividly recall the town of Livermore Falls. It was situated in the heart of the paper mill district; the river carrying logs flowed through the middle of town. The only attraction was the local restaurant, where they baked melt-in-your-mouth blueberry muffins every morning. As the summer wore on, Jack and I occasionally made the forty-five minute drive to Livermore Falls for our morning coffee and blueberry muffins, purchasing extras to take home.

Maine was glorious that summer, but we were so in love that anywhere would have been sensational. The cabin, buried deep in the woods near the tiny town of Fayette, could not have been more idyllic. It took Jack a week or so to regain his energy, but we were happy as two doves waltzing to Strauss' "Blue Danube Waltz." Like young lovers, we acted like two sea nymphs, enjoying our nakedness as we skinny dipped in the lake after dark. The loons often responded to our laughter. Two starved souls were suddenly awakened; it was a summer of ecstasy.

There were long unending conversations and discussions that had no answers. We cooked Maine lobsters and sautéed the largest sea scallops I had ever seen. We sailed the Atlantic with our friend, Peter. We went to clam bakes, made new friends, and entertained old ones. As if we had touched a bit of heaven, we would never forget our first summer together.

In June, the weather was cool with many rainy days–all good for barn sales, antiquing, eating lobster rolls, shopping for curtains and deck chairs, and making love. The days of July and August were sunny and warm for boating, fishing, and swimming, while the nights were cool for snuggling under blankets, listening to loons on the lake and raccoons rattling the trash can at three a.m.

Jack had purchased the lakefront property several years before. He and his boys had spent many hours renovating and making the cabin livable. Surrounded by pine trees, the original house had burned to the ground except for the chimney, which stood on the remaining deck, along with a small cabin–our home for the summer. Built of pine boards, the cabin had a picture window that looked out on the deck. Down the hill and through the trees, we could catch a glimmer of the lake.

The cabin was one large room with a small closet-like enclosure in one corner containing a lavatory, toilet, and shower stall. The kitchen in the adjacent corner was enclosed by bookcases. There were ample shelves for storage, and next to the sink was an apartment-size stove. A small refrigerator sat just outside the kitchen area. While space was limited, it filled our basic needs, and it was terribly romantic. We were like young newlyweds living in a third-floor walk-up in Greenwich Village. We savored every moment, and each day was more precious than the last.

To expand our cooking capacity, we invested in a ceramic crock pot and an electric broiler. Many mornings, I put dinner in the crock pot, enabling us to spend our days fishing, antiquing, or, when the spirit moved us, making love in the afternoons. Maybe dinner would be ham, green beans, potatoes, and onions, or a beef stew, or perhaps, a pot of chili on rainy days.

Jack had furnished the cabin with odds and ends picked up at barn sales and flea markets. On the opposite wall from the kitchen was a large bed. Wrapped tightly in each others arms, we slept there, warm and cozy. Mornings were cool, so we often started our days by lighting a fire in the fireplace. In front of the fireplace were two overstuffed chairs and a floor lamp for reading. Near the picture window was an old pine table, five or six feet in diameter, with assorted chairs, none of which matched.

We purchased a cotton braided rug and some colorful striped curtains for the windows. By summer's end, the cabin looked warm and inviting, like Jack and Nancy's place.

On the far side of the deck was a two-car garage made of old, faded gray slats of lumber. The front had been closed in with a door and screened windows. When Jack's boys, Bill, or guests came to visit, the garage–better known as the dormitory–was their sleeping quarters.

In the center of the room stood an old wood-burning stove and, around the periphery, were several iron bunk beds with their thin, lumpy mattresses. Warm blankets and pillows were piled on an old mahogany bureau in the far corner. With a fire burning in the stove, the dormitory was cozy and warm. In the dark of night, it was a great place for ghost stories.

Most summer people do not arrive in Maine until July, after the rainy season and black flies have passed. Jack and I felt like we owned a private country club with a secret entrance and a lake where you could see the shoreline for miles. We could actually stand on the dock and hear our voices reverberate from across the lake. For this reason, the lake was called Lake Echo. Occasionally, someone would pass in a small fishing boat or a speedboat, but the only people we talked to were the owners of the local country store in Fayette, fifteen miles west of Augusta, the state capitol.

Maine folk don't care much for outsiders, particularly summer people. Jack had been there several times during the previous fall and winter, so Joe and Maggie, owners of the country store, were a little more accepting of us. Never having left the state of Maine, they reminded me of characters in a Mark Twain novel. Wearing a housedress covered with faded flowers, probably made from old feed sacks, Maggie had tired, sad eyes peering out from her thin freckled face. Looking old before her time, when she smiled, it saddened me to look at the vacant spaces where her teeth should have been. She didn't talk much, only grinned and said, "good morning" or "howdy." Sometimes she didn't talk, but just filled our order.

When Jack and I went boating or fishing, we often took a couple of Maggie's delectable submarine sandwiches. Made fresh each morning and wrapped in white paper, the sandwiches were foot-long rolls of homemade bread filled with sliced ham or chicken, provolone cheese, sliced tomatoes, chopped green pepper and spring onions, all drizzled with vegetable oil. My mouth waters as I recall their unforgettable taste.

In contrast to Maggie's shyness, husband Joe, with bald head and beer belly, was a jolly, happy-go-lucky fellow who could talk with anyone about almost anything. Dressed in a white butcher's apron covered with the remains of some chicken or cow he had just carved, he always washed up before shaking hands with Jack. They could talk for hours about the weather, politics, fishing, summer people, and whether or not the world was going to hell.

Supplies at the country store were limited, so periodically we headed for Augusta, a metropolis in comparison to Fayette. Augusta was a small town with a population of 15,000. Over the summer, we discovered our favorite fish market, butcher shop, a wonderful hardware store, and we found a church home.

The Gothic-style Episcopal church with its sloping roof was very old and in need of repair. While we both were Presbyterian by heritage, we enjoyed the liturgy of the Episcopal, Lutheran, and Catholic churches, and felt comfortable in all. The congregation at the Episcopal Church appeared to be strait-laced, like Quakers or old Puritans who had lived there forever. Many of the older women wore long, dark-colored dresses, and covered their heads with bonnets tied under their chins.

We were attracted to this particular congregation by the warmth and generosity of the rector and his family. Following the service, on our first Sunday, the Reverend Harold Smithers welcomed us and introduced his attractive wife, Eunice, and two teenaged daughters. With brown eyes and a receding hairline circling his warm face, Harold looked as if he might have played football in his youth.

Eunice was tall, with hazel eyes and a crowning glory of soft curly brown hair. She had a trim frame with broad shoulders. Her radiant complexion, without a blemish, stands out in my memory, along with her genuine charm and old-fashioned hospitality.

Jack and I were instantly captivated by this couple. Before leaving the church that first Sunday, Harold and Eunice invited us for Sunday dinner, which was ready and waiting in the oven at the rectory next door.

What a wonderful afternoon. Thirty years later, my nostrils still recall the delicious aroma of roast beef au jus, mashed potatoes, and corn on the cob, wafting from the kitchen. Their two daughters flitted about, adding two more places at their walnut dining table, while Eunice blended an egg and flour batter, and heated an old iron skillet for preparing Yorkshire pudding. My first taste of the delicious English beef accompaniment melted on my tongue, almost instantly—as if it had vanished.

Dessert was fresh peach cobbler piled high with vanilla ice cream. The food, however, delicious as it was, was not a match for the stimulating conversation. Daughters Sarah and Katherine were beginning to think about college, so they asked many questions of Jack. Dark-haired Sarah was the older of the two. She was interested in music and theology. Katherine, with shimmering reddish-blond hair, had her mind set on being a biologist.

It was almost four o'clock before we said our goodbyes. We left feeling as if we had known the Smithers family forever. We became good friends and attended their church often when we were in Maine. We were frequent patrons of their all-you-could-eat-for-five-dollars church clambakes, held during July and August. One evening, the family joined us on our deck for lobster and sweet corn cooked in a big pot over an open fire. These special times would forever remain in my memory palace. Never could I have imagined that Harold would read the Scripture at Jack's funeral, five years later.

New friendships are refreshing and exciting, but it's the old friends who are always there for the good times, as well as for the trying times, and sometimes they show up when least expected. Our dear friend and colleague, Garrison Howard, suddenly, and to our great surprise, appeared on our deck in early August. Two years before, Garrison had resigned the deanship at Lindenwood and moved to Washington, D.C.

Finding his way to the Maine woods, he had inquired as to our whereabouts at the local country store. With his mop of white hair, stocky build, blue-gray eyes, and jovial sense of humor, Garrison loved to appear unannounced. We were delighted to see him. His visit was prompted by his wanting to see for himself the state of his mentor's health, and also wanting Jack's full accounting of the faculty situation at Lindenwood.

Warmed by the pot-bellied stove, Garrison had his own private quarters in the dormitory. Upon awakening each morning with the sun's rays streaming through the trees, the three of us began our days on the deck over steaming mugs of coffee and blueberry muffins from Livermore Falls, or Jack's famous pancakes.

We also shared with Garrison our love for Maine seafood, particularly scallops and lobster. One day, we drove into Augusta to have a lobster roll for lunch. Served on bread similar to a hot dog bun, and filled with mounds of lobster salad, it was luscious beyond description. On our way home, we stopped at a roadside market and picked up a pound of fresh sea scallops, Country Gentleman corn, homegrown tomatoes, and blackberries for our supper.

Jack could turn any meal into a banquet—no matter how meager the selection. In fact, it was from him I learned the importance of making each meal special, whether it's for family or friends, on a weekday or Sunday. On that particular evening, he grilled the scallops, I cooked corn and sliced the tomatoes, and Garrison made the martinis. The scallops, browned in butter and sautéed with chopped celery and onions, were so succulent that we ate the whole pound in one sitting. We dined by candlelight on the deck, listening to the loons and crickets.

For four days, we talked, went boating and fishing, laughed, cooked lobsters, drank wine, and shared stories long into the night. Our conversations were unending and seamless. While we would remember this time with fondness, the joy of Garrison's visit would be forever overshadowed by the catastrophic event that followed.

On Monday morning, it was time for Jack to make his weekly call to Sally and Maria, his devoted secretaries. Maria had worked twenty-five years for the former president, and seven years with Jack; Sally had been a part of the team for five years. Both women anxiously awaited Jack's call that morning.

Because there was no phone at the cabin, when we needed to make a call, we drove a deserted country road to the only phone booth within a five mile radius of our cabin. Normally, I accompanied Jack and called my office staff as well, but Garrison insisted on joining Jack that morning.

An hour later they returned to the cabin and Jack fell on to a deck chair, reeling from the incredulous phone conversation. His expression was a mask of disbelief. His face was drawn with a ghost-like pallor; his blue eyes had turned the grey of cigar smoke. Dripping with perspiration, he shared the devastating phone conversation, while Garrison paced the deck, shaking his head–not believing the incomprehensible message that had rocked Jack to his very core.

Jack had talked with Sally and learned that Regis Herrold, the chairman of the college's board of trustees, wished to speak with him. Jack immediately called Regis. Although they had a good working relationship, Regis was recognized among his peers for his arrogant demeanor and overbearing personality.

By the end of their conversation, Jack was slumped and speechless on the floor of the phone booth. In direct opposition to the unanimous support Jack had received from the board two months earlier, Regis had now asked for his resignation. As if he had been stabbed with a sword, Jack was not only shocked and angry, but he felt betrayed; maybe, in his absence, someone had been undermining him. We would never know, but I believe a colleague, aspiring to be president, deserted his colleague and longtime friend. After our departure from Lindenwood, we never heard from that colleague again.

While Jack had planned to resign the following May, he'd wanted the coming academic year to balance the budget and make amends with disgruntled faculty. The sudden eruption of our lives threw us into an emotional tailspin. Believing things happen for a reason, I was convinced God had deliberately sent Garrison to be a counselor to us during this awful time. Jack and I might have made impromptu decisions without thinking them through, had Garrison's level-headed advice not prevailed.

After hours of discussion, we decided to allay any rumors by having me return to the campus as soon as possible. Garrison would stay in Maine a few more days, assisting Jack however he could. Jack would drive home within the week. Our plans to fly Bill to Maine for the last week in August were tossed aside. I never imagined my departure would be so abrupt; my emotions were raw.

Early the next morning, Jack and Garrison deposited me at the Augusta airport, a small facility with only one runway and one airplane, the Flying Goose, with its eight seats. Departure was more than difficult. After two glorious months, how could I possibly leave Jack? I was eager to see my son, but saying goodbye to Jack was one of the most troubling moments of my life.

Jack and I would be together again within the week, but a year or more would pass before Garrison reentered our lives. In the meantime, there were unexpected challenges, dreams that came to fruition, and a multitude of new friends, but our friendship with Garrison would always be there.

Then, suddenly, the dream Jack and I had of sharing our lives with students and faculty at Muskingum College came to a shattering halt, and I was faced with the prospect of losing him. I was fighting for every heart beat, while my conscious mind told me death was a possibility. Life-altering situations take all the courage, grit, and grace you can muster. Only the strong survive, so they say.

As I lay in the dark that night, watching the snow flakes freeze on the window, I wondered who the strong were. Depleted of all energy, my exhausted body and outraged mind would not let me sleep. Maybe I would freeze on the window.

No doubt, I had a few hours when my brain shut down, but that didn't stop the nightmares. As Mahatma Gandhi once wrote, "Each night, when I go to sleep, I die. And the next morning, when I wake up, I am reborn." If Jack awoke in the morning, I knew God wanted him to live another day. One day at a time. I defiantly refused to believe Jack's disease was not reversible.

The challenge was never the possibility of death. It was how to stop the debilitating effects of cardiomyopathy that depleted Jack's heart muscle, cell by cell. Did the doctors really believe they could save his life, or were they just prolonging the inevitable? Without the biopsy, they really didn't know.

Day 3

Shortly after daybreak, I gathered my bed clothes and deposited them in my locker before I rushed to see Jack. Awake and alert he glared at me as if to say, "What have they done to me?" He couldn't talk with the respirator tube protruding from his throat. Fear was written across his face; I squeezed his cold hands between mine. My heart cried silently. There were so many tubes, along with a plastic tent covering his upper body, that I couldn't even kiss him. The nurses were trying to keep the germs away, but he looked like he had been stored for safe-keeping.

Jack was terrified by the gurgling of the respirator, the tube in his throat, and his inability to talk. He had a fear of strokes. I tried to assure him that he had not suffered a stroke; he shook his head as if he didn't believe me. There was no doubt in my mind that Dr. Sumner's comment about blood clots had contributed to his fear. I felt completely helpless to subdue his anxiety, much less elevate his spirits.

I sat in the recliner by Jack's bed, held his hand, and gently massaged his body for most of that day. Trying to keep my strength up, when my tummy growled or when Jack was sleeping, I slipped away to the coffee shop. Life was timeless, so there was no rhyme or reason to my meals. It was difficult to believe my powerful husband was panic-stricken, like a child, and it was impossible to leave him alone, unless one of the nurses was there.

That morning, after one of the LPNs arrived to give him his bath and change the bed linens, I assured Jack of my return. Then, I hurried to the coffee shop for a quick blueberry muffin, orange juice, and coffee. Before doing so, I stepped into the drugstore and picked up a morning paper, the *St. Louis Globe-Democrat*, one of my favorite newspapers at the time. I knew I could not long maintain my sanity in the ICU, where minutes, hours, and days melted into each other, if I didn't know what was going on in the outside world.

As Jack lay helpless surrounded by tubes, hanging bottles, and the ever-pumping respirator, he also had to endure numerous blood tests and transfusions. As every bag of someone else's blood slowly became part of my husband's body, I was fearful that it would further weaken his condition, or give him some other terrible disease.

To my horror, before the day was over, Jack developed irregular heart beats, his breathing became labored, and perspiration flowed. He had reacted to the Digitalis, which was supposed to improve the pumping action and regulate the beat of his heart. In addition to the toxicity problem, the Lasix, which emptied excess fluid from his body, caused malfunction of the kidneys. It was a long, tough day.

Jack's life was on the line. He knew it, and I knew it. He was locked in a nightmare, fighting for his life–and unable to talk–while I was emotionally drained, almost catatonic, but truly scared. We held on to each other for dear life; our eyes, no doubt, told the story. I knew it was going to take one of God's miracles to survive this battle.

Jack struggled for every breath, while the cardiac care area filled to capacity with other desperately ill patients. With anguished expressions and free-flowing tears, friends and relatives came and went from "my room" all day. I met my parents there in the early afternoon. They were shocked to learn that Jack was on a respirator, and to find me so distraught. I paced the floor, unable to sit. Realizing it was not a good day for me, Mother and Daddy were gone by mid afternoon.

Shortly after their departure, a familiar face appeared at Jack's door. Jeanette Pennywaite, a graduate of Lindenwood College, was to be his CVP–cardio-ventricular pulmonary specialist. Looking like a basketball player at almost six feet, Jeanette had long, auburn hair tied in a pony tail. Her captivating eyes were a rich emerald green, like a cat's.

Embarrassed as he was for a former student to see him ill, Jack managed to acknowledge her presence with a smile. From that day on, Jeanette came daily to massage Jack's chest. Using the side of her hand, she would gently pound up and down his rib cage, loosening the phlegm in his lungs. It was an exhausting procedure for Jack; when it was over, he always instantly fell asleep.

By early evening, the waiting room had cleared and only one visitor remained. Her name was Mrs. Baker, and her husband had been admitted with a massive heart attack. From a rural community in southern Illinois, they were hard-working farm folk; her husband had never been sick a day in his life. Mrs. Baker appeared to be in her early seventies. Her bobbed white hair silhouetted the weathered skin of her face. She was overcome with grief and worry, but we briefly shared our stories.

I observed Mrs. Baker's pillow and blanket; it appeared I was going to share my private room. Sleep would be difficult. Like a lawn mower plowing through grass, Mrs. Baker snored long into the night. Jack was knocked out, so I paced the corridors.

After most of the patients had gone to sleep and things quieted down in the ICU, sometime after one o'clock, I chatted with several of the nurses: Sylvia and Juanita, a Creole LPN, with an enchanting smile and glistening ivory teeth.

Juanita had been a cardiac nurse for fifteen years. She knew the ropes and heartaches of her patients. After Jack had been at St. Luke's the previous fall, he wrote about Juanita in his newspaper column:

> ...When a group of medical students and residents crowded into my room and began to make indiscreet remarks about the way things were going, she leaned over my bed and whispered in my ear a comforting statement: "They don't know what they're talking about. You're just an interesting case and you're going to be alright, honey..."

Finally, there was twenty-five year old Brenda, the youngest, with less than two years' nursing experience. With an auspicious goal of serving in the Peace Corps, someday she would make a great contribution to a medical team in the underprivileged world.

My new friends went out of their way to be helpful and accommodate my every need. They made me feel like I belonged, as they talked about the stress of taking care of critically ill cardiac patients, and the difficulties and frustrations with the administration of the ICU. This was before the advent of the computer, so they felt overburdened with the detailed paper work that had to be entered into each patient's chart. Sylvia shared with me that six weeks was the longest she could endure the stress. She routinely escaped to the beach for at least a week and sometimes longer.

That evening, occasionally interrupted by one of their patients, my new friends rambled on as long as I listened. Before saying goodnight, Sylvia suggested I might want to read about cardiomyopathy in one of their reference books.

Unable to sleep with the distraction of Mrs. Baker's snoring, I curled up with my pillow and a book entitled *Diseases of the Heart.*

While the subject matter was not entertaining, I was on a quest to learn everything about the heart muscle and the unknown viruses which sometimes attack its center. If I was to be there indefinitely, I might as well educate myself, I thought. Like reading a Greek tragedy, I turned the pages long into the night, until my blood shot eyes closed like an automatic door.

Day 4

Around 4:30 a.m., I was awakened by Sylvia. She momentarily scared me out of my wits. Wanting to know if he could talk, Jack had pulled the respirator tube, and then thought I should know, too. The doctors on call decided to see how he would do without the respirator, but by 9:00 a.m., they had to replace it. His body slowly filled with fluid again and he was exhausted.

Dr. Poole returned and talked with me about performing peritoneal dialysis, a last-ditch effort, in his opinion. Tears looming, I took a deep breath, counting to ten. It was another defining moment that required a pivotal decision. Again, there was no choice. The only decision turned out to be the right decision.

The next seventeen hours were a gripping journey, carefully orchestrated by a terrific medical team. An enormous circular machine filled Jack's body with water through a long plastic tube inserted into his abdomen. The tubing cycled back into the dialysis machine, where the toxins were flushed out. The cleansed fluid was then returned to the abdomen.

Each cycle of the apparatus required an hour, and there were seventeen cycles. Each time, more water came out than initially had been inserted, dispelling a greater volume of infection, as well. Purifying the water in Jack's body was a transforming symbolic experience for me, and a critical turning point in my husband's life.

My hours were spent massaging Jack's hand, meditating, and praying. Taking a break, I sometimes made my way to the hospital chapel. Located in a quiet corner on the first floor, the chapel was a small, dimly lit room dominated by a beautiful hand-carved birch wood altar surrounded by a white and gold-gilded railing and maroon velvet kneeling cushions. The wall behind the altar was draped in the same plush material, pleated from ceiling to floor.

A majestic pewter cross hung by a long chain directly over the altar. While the meditation book and hymnals indicated St.

Luke's was affiliated with the Episcopal Church, people of all faiths were invited to use the chapel.

As I entered the quiet alcove, the only light shone directly over the altar. There was one other person there–a young woman kneeling in the first row of the three pews that flanked each side of the aisle. Sobbing, she held her head in her hands. I wondered who she was, and if someone in her family was dying. Seeking the solace of God's spirit myself, I was too racked with pain and fear to comfort her.

That day, my mind had been hypnotized by the water gently flowing in and out of Jack's body. I found myself thinking about the use of water for healing. Across the history of Christianity, the history of the Jewish faith, as well as many Eastern religions, there is a definitive spiritual significance to the cleansing power of water.

From the earliest days, water has been used for baptism and cleansing from sin. Jesus, a devout Jew, was baptized by John.

Later, Christ washed the feet of his disciples, and washing the hands and feet have been a meaningful custom among the Jewish, Middle Eastern, and Far Eastern peoples. "Frequent purification of the person is taken as symbolic of spiritual cleansing under the Mosaic Law. To offer facilities for the washing of hands and feet is one of the recognized rites of Eastern hospitality." *The Bible Reader's Encyclopædia and Concordance*, Revised Edition, p.393, published by Collins' Clear-Type Press, London and New York.

There are numerous references in the Bible to the cleansing and healing power of water:

> *He leads me beside the still waters; he restores my soul.*
> (Psalms 23:2)
> *Wash me, and I shall be whiter than snow."*
> (Psalms 51:7)
> *Then he poured water into a basin, and began to wash the disciples' feet, and to wipe them with the towel with which he was girded.*
> (John 13:5)
> *Christ loved the church and gave himself up for her, that he might sanctify her, having cleansed her by the washing of water with the word.*
> (Ephesians 5:25-26)

Kneeling in the chapel that afternoon, I prayed Jack's body would be healed through the gallons and gallons of water flushed through his body. As in the Twenty-third Psalm, I prayed his soul would be restored. Leaving the chapel after more than an hour of solitude, I felt refreshed and amazingly peaceful.

I returned to the ICU to find that one of our favorite people, Maria Fhosha, had come to see Jack. When he'd been hospitalized the previous September, Dr. Fhosha was the resident physician responsible for his care. Dr. Fhosha always called him, "John" and she was "Maria" to him. Born and educated in India, Maria was charming, as well as beautiful, with long, coal-black hair often twisted into a bun. Her colorful, flowered pink and green sari peeked out from beneath her white lab coat. On this visit, I was shocked to see her in a wheel chair.

Maria was scheduled for lumbar spine surgery, and had a private room several floors above. What a wonderful surprise when she graciously invited me to use her shower during my stay at the hospital. A miracle had descended.

Following Jack's successful dialysis, he was resting comfortably, while I was feeling like a dog that had rolled in the grass and needed to get rid of an itch. I escaped to take a shower, my first since leaving home several days earlier. After three of the most miserable days of my life, I was able to heal and refresh my own body with water.

Standing under the cascading hot water, with my eyes closed, I visualized three days worth of oil and dirt flowing from my head to my toes and down the drain pipe. After what seemed like an hour, I emerged, revitalized with renewed energy to face whatever lay ahead. Toweling my hair dry, I donned a crimson-colored Muskingum College sweatshirt and charcoal gray slacks. Strange, but I was dressed for bed. I could have worn my bathrobe, but if anyone had seen me, they might have mistaken me for a patient and wondered what I was doing wandering the halls.

Opening the bathroom door, I found Maria reading. I was too tired to talk, so I simply said thank you and goodnight. She smiled and wished me a restful night's sleep. While suffering from excruciating back pain, she looked radiant, like a princess in her pink silk pajamas and her flowing black hair draped over her shoulders.

Maria's private room became my escape hatch where I retreated many evenings. No matter how depressed I was, a warm shower and conversation with Maria always energized me. It was emotionally satisfying to have woman talk with someone who understood the effects of Jack's condition. She spoke carefully, once saying, "I wish I could think of ten words that would make you feel good." She would never know how she calmed my nerves.

Through Maria's friendship, I came to a better understanding of Jack's disease, and was better able to cope with the situation. How could I ever repay her kindness? I hoped I could be of help to her following her surgery.

Ready to face the world after my shower that evening, I checked on a sleeping Jack. All the lights had been turned off and the only illumination glowed from the heart monitor over his bed. Although he was still on the respirator, his breathing seemed less raspy and more even. So as not to wake him, I gently kissed his cheek, left the door slightly ajar, and checked with one of the nurses to confirm all was well for the moment.

Sylvia was taking a much needed night off and Brenda was in charge. With her closely cropped black hair under the nurse's cap, Brenda had deep blue, penetrating eyes set in a round, perky, smiling face. Short in stature, but long in caring, she promised to wake me if problems arose during the night.

Unless there was an emergency, the late night hours in a hospital took on an eerie ghost-like feeling. Lights were dimmed and the only sounds were occasional footsteps of the medical staff. Initially, I was uncomfortable, but eventually came to relish the peace and quiet. On that particular evening, I settled into the empty waiting room, taking the morning paper to a lounge chair in the far corner. Later, after checking on Jack, I retrieved my pillow and blanket from the nurses' lounge with the hope of being able to sleep after reading a few more pages.

My shoulder bag contained most everything I needed, including a paperback written by one of my favorite fiction writers, Barbara Taylor Bradford. Her *Woman of Substance* gave me strength, as I related to the courage and persistence of the female characters. After reading awhile, my eyes slammed shut. I slept a full seven hours for the first time in three days.

Much to the surprise of the medical team, Jack survived nine days on the respirator and the seventeen hours of peritoneal dialysis. As the minutes and hours rolled by, Jack became more restful. However, his blood pressure dropped, and his fluctuating heart rate continued to keep everyone in a state of tension. All I could do was hope and pray that the treatment would have a long-term positive effect. Faith would carry us through. There was never a doubt in my mind that Jack would survive cardiac intensive care, and so would I.

Chapter IV

A QUESTION OF FAITH

"Take the first step in faith. You don't have to see the whole staircase, just take the first step."
—*Dr. Martin Luther King, Jr.*

Day 5 - 8

The peritoneal dialysis was successful, but the road to recovery was fraught with barriers. The possibility of pneumonia or other bacterial infection loomed on the horizon. So life in suspension continued, and survival depended on Jack's will to live, the doctors' expertise, and God's healing power. His survival would require all the patience, faith, and prayer I could muster. The days ahead were going to be long, and the nights even longer.

Jack was without the tubes of the dialysis machine, but the respirator continued to breathe for him. Oh, how he hated that monstrosity that inhibited his ability to communicate. I shared my telephone conversations and tried to assure him everything was taken care of at home and at the college. However, I was not always sure how much he comprehended. Being unable to talk was so frustrating that he often became irritable. Finally, one evening, Sylvia fetched a chalk board, saving the day.

Jack occasionally wrote a short question, or an "I love you," but he was so weak that even writing was difficult. Fortunately, his heart rate decreased and his "lungs were remarkably clear," according to x-ray reports. He slept a great deal, while I found myself increasingly frustrated and impatient. Even if he survived, I wondered whether he would be the vibrant man I knew and loved. I prayed for patience, patience, and more patience.

My days took on a new rhythm. At last, Jack was sleeping through the night, and so was I. I awoke each morning to the sound of squeaky rubber-soled shoes, as student nurses began their day. Though I didn't mind being awakened, I really didn't like hearing their chatter at that hour of the morning, usually around six-thirty.

During the time of crisis I had no trouble arising. I was on the move when my feet hit the floor. Each morning I quickly ran a brush through my hair and was off to say good morning to

Jack. Generally, he was awake and wondering where I had been all night. He was so confused. After a kiss and big hug, I washed his face with a warm washcloth, and combed his salt-and-pepper hair, which was getting whiter with each passing day. If he appeared to be emotionally stable and in a good mood, I headed for the locker room to brush my teeth, wash my face, apply fresh make-up, and change clothes. If not, I remained unkempt until nightfall.

The nurses' locker room, much like a large walk-in-closet, was a drab place with gray steel lockers lining the walls, and several worn wooden benches. There was a double sink and cabinets at one end of the room. A rectangular mirror hung over the counter-top, but the lighting was poor and it was difficult to see, certainly not the ideal place for applying make-up. Most of the time, I looked haggard and, obviously, I had lost weight. I wasn't especially eager to look at myself.

In spite of how I felt, it was important to look as attractive as I could for Jack. The early morning was the only opportunity, until late at night, to do anything for myself. Each morning, after redressing in one of the five outfits I had with me, I walked the long corridor to the elevator and headed for the hospital coffee shop.

Following breakfast, grand rounds took place anytime between nine and eleven; they involved anywhere from five to eight doctors, residents, interns, and medical students. I never knew exactly what time they would arrive, nor did I know how long they would deliberate. Dr. Rainey, with his shock of white hair, black eyebrows, and wire-rimmed glasses, led the discussion. In his heavily starched white lab coat, looking serious and intent, Dr. Rainey presented a brief summary of Jack's situation, followed by questions and comments from the medical staff. Occasionally, the chief exhibited a sense of humor, with a twinkle in his eye.

The first few days of grand rounds, Jack was irritated by so many people surrounding his bed. No doubt he felt closed in and claustrophobic. As time went on, however, he seemed to look forward to their visits. It was a true learning experience for me, and became an opportunity to ask questions. There were times when I heard things I really didn't want to know, such as frightening statistics about cardiomyopathy and specific details about Jack's condition.

I learned that, without a biopsy of the heart muscle, the doctors were unable to indicate a prognosis. Even today, Jack might or might not have been eligible for a heart transplant. The one piece of good news was that he had successfully survived peritoneal dialysis; now, if they could only get him off that damned respirator.

By the time grand rounds were over, it was time for more tests. Every single day it was more tests, followed by the morning sponge bath. By then, Jack would be so exhausted he'd sleep until time for lunch, such as it was. As long as he was on the respirator, all foods were liquid nutrients, received intravenously. Some days he would sleep right through lunch. I would take the opportunity to get a quick salad or sandwich, read the morning paper, or make phone calls, until my parents arrived in the early afternoon.

I would be forever indebted for my parents' daily visits. However, they had no business driving, much less walking on the ice and snow. As I looked from the window of the coffee shop, I could see mountains of snow everywhere. It never stopped snowing long enough for the sidewalks to be cleared.

Some afternoons, the minister of my parents' church, Dr. Eli Benjamin, would stop to have a few minutes of prayer with Jack. A handsome fifty-year-old with graying hair and a rotund silhouette, he always wore a dark suit with a clerical collar. I didn't know Dr. Benjamin well, but he and my parents were dear friends, and I appreciated his loving concern. At times, Jack acknowledged his presence, and other times, he was completely unaware or sleeping.

The pattern of my days seldom varied. An observer might have said they were monotonous, with an occasional crisis thrown in to relieve the boredom. I had one mission: to help Jack recover. Each day, after my parents' departure, I sat at Jack's bedside into the late afternoon and early evening. Somewhere along the way, I had a light supper and, hopefully, a chat with Dr. Rainey. After my evening phone calls, if I was lucky, my day ended with the long-awaited shower and chat with Maria.

I was grateful that Jack showed signs of improvement, and that I was allowed to spend every hour and every minute with him. Other families were not so lucky. Over the previous weekend, code blue calls were frequent; three ICU patients died. Fortunately, Jack appeared to be stable. Dr. Rainey came every day, sometimes late at night; I wondered if the man ever slept.

I also pondered what might have happened had we opted to stay in our local hospital in Ohio, which didn't have the latest technology for cardiac care. I knew only that we were more comfortable with Dr. Rainey, a highly respected cardiologist, not only in the United States, but also in the international medical community. We had known him for many years and trusted his judgment.

After a lifetime of observing patients and the medical profession, I have become critically aware of the importance one's doctor plays in a life-threatening situation. I believe you must place absolute trust and faith in his or her hands. Along with your faith in God, or another higher power, there is no other choice when your life is at stake. It is best if the relationship is fostered in times of relative good health, so that if a whirlwind descends, you have one less worry. You don't have to search for a new doctor, and learn to trust again in a time of crisis.

Day 9

On the morning of the ninth day, January 23, the respirator was disconnected and the suction tube removed. Hoarse as Jack was, his words were music to my ears, "I love you," he whispered. Tears rolled from my eyes and splashed on Jack's face as I leaned to kiss him. Sylvia cried, too. She wanted to move him to the recliner. I thought it was too soon. She insisted that Jack must sit in an upright position, in order to breathe correctly and cough up any phlegm that might be blocking his throat.

With the departure of the respirator, seven of the hanging bottles also disappeared. After twenty minutes, Jack was coughing and his voice became extremely hoarse. The activity had been too much. The pendulum had swung again. Atrial fibrillation returned, galloping at full speed.

Suddenly, out of the blue, Dr. Poole rushed into the room and yelled at one of the nurses, "No depressants! This is a miracle here. Let's not lower the blood pressure. He can live with fibrillation." That was good news to my ears. But by nightfall, five of the hanging bottles were back in place. I wrote in my journal, "Oh dear God, he is so weak. It is indeed going to be a very long road to recovery."

Initially, and much to his consternation, Jack could have only ice, no water. He was so thirsty, having had no food or water for nine days. I fed him ice throughout the day and, finally, by evening, he was able to quench his thirst with a drink of water. His first swallow was followed by a deep sigh.

As he became increasingly aware of what was going on around him, Jack asked me who was moaning in the next room. I told him it was a confused black woman who'd had one of her legs amputated and then suffered a heart attack. The male patient on the other side was suffering from massive blood clots.

Jack was the most embarrassed I had ever seen him when his morning nurse, Tamara Mason, told him he would have to use a bed pan now that the catheter had been removed. In spite of how sick he was, Jack still had his sense of humor. With a twinkle in his eye, he called the bed pan his sugar scoop. Tamara laughed, and so did I. I couldn't remember the last time I had laughed; it felt so good.

Tamara was a delightful young woman. A radiant glow surrounded her face when she spoke. I truly believe she was blessed with the Holy Spirit. Before Tamara went off duty that day, she recited a beautiful prayer for Jack: "Lord, hold him in the palm of your hand," and then wished us goodnight.

Jack, feeling blessed and relaxed, drifted off to sleep. I hoped he would have pleasant dreams, because he'd had scary nightmares while on the respirator. Within a few minutes he was snoring. I stole away for some quiet time.

Quiet was short-lived with the addition of a new roommate, Mrs. Kable. A robust woman and mother of ten, she was a talker. Her husband had suffered a massive myocardial infarction--a heart attack. She wasn't sure he was going to make it. I tried to write in my journal, but Mrs. Kable wanted to talk, and so I listened. It was the least I could do.

A short time later, I was rescued by Jeanette Pennywaite. She graciously invited me to join her for dinner. The conversation was refreshing and I enjoyed her company.

Jeanette had a brilliant mind to go with her charming personality. I was stunned to learn of her recent divorce. However, this should not have come as a surprise. She had fallen prey to what I called the L.C. syndrome. While I served as alumnni director at Lindenwood College (L.C.), I was shocked at the high percentage of graduates who were divorced, myself included. Most of us were from small towns in the Midwest, and had been raised to believe in the sanctity of the home and family. Yet, thousands of us had left our first husbands behind and struck out on our own.

Jeanette and I did not discuss this proclivity for divorce over dinner, but we did talk about Jack's unstable condition, our life at Muskingum College, and Jeanette's future career plans. She was attending Washington University Medical School with the ultimate goal of becoming a cardiologist. Often, I have wondered what became of Jeanette. Perhaps our paths will cross at an alumni gathering someday.

Following the enjoyable dinner and conversation, I checked on the still-sleeping Jack. He needed all the rest he could get, so I was off to my phone booth for a quick call to Bill and David. The telephone was ringing as I approached; Garrison Howard was on the line. He had tried to reach Jack at his office only to learn that we had taken up residence in St. Louis. I was overjoyed to hear his voice.

Garrison was always there for us during traumatic times. When students were dismissed for covering up an abortion, he was there; and when Jack collapsed in the phone booth on a lonely Down East road, Garrison was there.

His telephone call sent my mind flooding back to the weeks following that unsettling episode. I had not seen Garrison since that morning he and Jack deposited me at the airport for my solo journey to St. Louis.

After embracing Garrison and Jack, with tears rolling down my cheeks, I gave Jack a lingering, wet kiss, then ascended the steps, waved goodbye, and boarded the Flying Goose. The two pilots in their neatly pressed navy trousers, white shirts, and midnight blue ties were already on board along with two other passengers, a businessman in his grey flannel suit and a young woman dressed in a navy pin-striped suit, probably a flight attendant on the way to her next job.

My heart was missing Jack already, but the thirty-minute flight was glorious. There was not a cloud in the sky, and the morning sun cast a brilliant glow on the gigantic waves that pounded against the huge boulders lining the coastline.

After a short flight, the plane landed in Boston and I made my way through throngs of travelers to board a 747 to St. Louis. To my left sat a ghostly-looking man whose rugged profile reminded me of Basil Rathbone, as did his deep voice. He tried to strike up a conversation, but I was not interested. I was locked in a cocoon, trying to figure out what had happened, and where Jack and I were going. Our discussions had been difficult, but I believed Jack and I had come to terms with reality rather quickly.

We would not be living in the president's house at Lindenwood, but we were where we wanted to be, and that was together. Early in the summer, my gut instinct had told me we should leave Lindenwood. It would be best, because Jack did not need such a stressful environment. I also wanted our lives together to begin in another place, not at my alma mater, and not where Jack had been president. Our personal relationships with many of the faculty and administration were special, and should be remembered as they were. I will always believe that was God's plan.

Where we would live remained a question mark. Temporarily, we resided at my home. Our plans to move couldn't be completed until we formally resigned our positions, wiping the slate clean, and giving us time to think and plan.

With the plane on its final approach to Lambert Airport in St. Louis, it was time to shift my focus. I was excited to see Bill and my parents. Entering the congested airport, I picked up my luggage and headed for the departure gate. Immediately, I spotted my handsome son, my bald-headed father, and my mother with a twinkle in her eyes. Hugging Bill, with his straggly teenage hair, I couldn't believe how much he had grown in only a few months.

At thirteen, he obviously was in a real growth spurt. I anticipated eventually he would be as tall, if not taller, than his father who was six-feet-four. Conversation was non-stop as we drove the thirty minutes to my Kirkwood home. Bill had had a wonderful summer playing baseball, swimming, and fishing with his dad. Doting grandparents took him to the zoo and St. Louis Cardinal Baseball games. I was pleased, for it eased any guilt feelings I might have had.

The following morning, I turned to thoughts of the college and my responsibilities as admissions director. Wondering how my colleagues would react to my new persona as "Mrs. Brown," I arrived at my office unannounced. Good news greeted me. Applications and deposit payments for the freshman class showed an increase over the previous year. I congratulated my staff on a job well done.

They welcomed me back with hugs and congratulations on my marriage to Jack. Everyone was in a mood to celebrate, so one of the work-study students went for doughnuts. I had yet to share my news, so no one had any idea that Jack and I were resigning our positions.

We enjoyed our coffee and doughnuts, and then, I announced that Jack and I were leaving. My staff was shocked. Two of my assistants, Beth

Lonneman and Barry Vandergill, were visibly upset; tears stood in their eyes. Beth loved Jack as if he were her father; and she considered me her mentor. Years later, she became a director of admissions and, eventually, the vice president for development at a Virginia college. I was proud of her success and we kept in touch for many years.

Pleased to be representing the college after his graduation, Barry had been a recruit in the first class of eight men. Barry, too, became a successful business person and president of his own company. Years later, at an alumni reunion weekend, I almost didn't recognize him. His hair had turned snow-white before his fortieth birthday. Beth and Barry stayed at Lindenwood for several more years before they, too, moved on.

By telephone, Jack relayed a similar message about our departure to his secretaries, Maria and Sally. We had timed our announcement, so that the news would hit the campus at the same time. No official notice of our resignations was made public until Jack returned from Maine.

He called me every evening that week. I pictured him with his flashlight in the cramped phone booth on the deserted country road. Our conversations were lengthy; I never wanted to return the phone to its cradle. Jack spent the week boarding up our cabin for the winter, and left on Saturday for the long drive home. When he walked into my office on Monday, I was overjoyed.

Grinning from ear to ear, he picked me up, and swirled me around the room. He was unusually happy and relaxed. At that moment, I knew our departure from Lindenwood was the right decision.

The next day we mailed our letters of resignation to Regis Herrold. In response, the board gave Jack a severance package: one year's salary and his college car, a burgundy-colored Oldsmobile. Since Jack paid substantial alimony to his former wife, and I would no longer have a full-time salary, our financial life would have been in dire straits without the compensation.

We completed unfinished tasks, cleared our desks, and packed our memorabilia during the ensuing weeks. I would miss my office. Three large-paned windows flooded the room with light, singling out my circular walnut desk, a multi-colored tweed sofa, coffee table, and several occasional chairs. The spacious room was ideal for interviewing students and their parents. Sadly, I thought, I would not be doing that anymore.

Jack's office was decorated with his unique style. The rich red carpet set the stage for the immense room with its huge dark mahogany desk and antique hutch filled with books and his inkwell collection. He had discovered the hutch, covered with dust, buried in the attic of the administration building. At one time, it had held laboratory equipment in the chemistry department. Waxed to a warm luster, the massive hutch, eight feet in length, added an elegant ambience to the space.

In another part of the room sat two black-and-white print Chippendale sofas, several occasional tables, and an antique brass-hinged, gate-legged coffee table. Several oil paintings and watercolors completed the décor.

Before our relationship had entered the public domain, in late afternoons we occasionally snatched a half-hour alone in Jack's office or mine, before I headed for home. Yes, we would miss the place, but more than the place, we would miss our friends and colleagues.

Parting was difficult. There was Harry, the art historian, whom we loved dearly; Paul, the painter with red hair and a neatly trimmed beard, who reminded me of Vincent Van Gogh; Kate, the psychology professor, who was truly disappointed that we were leaving; and numerous others we would never forget.

Perhaps, the saddest person was Ulysses, a tall, jovial black man who had worked at the college for more than twenty-five years. Always elegantly dressed in his white jacket, black tie, and black trousers, he had served as the butler to two presidents. We never saw Ulysses again, but he called me at the hospital when Jack was dying.

Along with tears of joy and sadness, there were farewell luncheons, dinners, and a reception where our colleagues presented us with a fluted silver tray inscribed, "From Your Friends at Lindenwood."

On a sun-drenched September afternoon, similar to the day we met, we exited the administration building hand-in-hand, never to return. Jack was proud of the new vision of academic reform that had been implemented during his tenure. He had given his best, and so had I. Now, new and unknown challenges would present themselves.

As Jack and I planned our future, we knew my house, with its three small bedrooms and one bath, would not suffice for a growing teenager and our menagerie to which Sandy, Jack's Collie, had been added. We put my house on the market and found an appealing four-bedroom, brick ranch on a spacious property, located a mile from Bill's junior high school. Our new home was perfect, a symbol for our new life together.

Since I was no longer employed, I wondered what I would do with my time, but I soon found out. We packed the contents of two houses, moved from each on the same day, organized our belongings into one household, cleaned my former house before selling and, last, had a garage sale. Some of the furniture in the president's house was owned by the college, but there were many pieces, and most of the art work, that belonged to Jack.

On moving day, we began at the president's house, loading Jack's personal furnishings and possessions, and then the moving van went to my home. Hiding behind boxes and under sofas, our pets watched with fear and trepidation, no doubt afraid of being packed in some box, or left behind.

Decorating our new abode was a joy, although Jack's and my furniture was of different vintages: antiques, early American, and a few contemporary pieces. The eclectic blend made for an interesting challenge. We had carefully selected the pieces we wished to keep, and every room was brimming over. I reclaimed the antique bed I had slept in as a teenager, and that my mother had sold to a friend. A walnut bed with an eight-foot headboard, circa 1840, originally from my mother's family in Tennessee, came home to stay. Our first furniture purchase was a walnut chest-of-drawers, also an antique, to complement our bed in the master bedroom.

My Thomasville fruitwood hutch, table, and chairs occupied our dining room, and the living room held Jack's furniture, including two loveseats, a baby grand piano, and an antique grandfather clock. Spacious with white walls, a fireplace, and two large windows looking out on the backyard and woods beyond, the family room came to life with the addition of red tweed pillows and cushions on the sofa, and an oval braided, multicolored rug.

Needless to say, Bill enjoyed having his own private bath, enabling him to shower as long as he wished. He certainly gave new meaning to a long shower, with absolutely no thought to the cost of water flowing down the drain.

The transition to a new home, along with a new stepfather, was difficult for Bill, but he slowly began to enjoy being a teenager. He saw his old friends at school, made new friends in the neighborhood, and saw his dad on weekends.

Life was good. Jack and I experienced great happiness and found a new sense of freedom to be who we were, instead of what was expected. We savored the privacy. We laughed; we cried tears of joy; we hung pictures, and mopped floors; we cooked in our spacious kitchen, making soup and chopping onions; and, we entertained friends, talking long into the night.

We went to St. Louis Symphony concerts, and boated with friends on the Missouri River. On one occasion, Jack got carried away by his new sense of freedom and deliberately jumped into the river. He disappeared with the undercurrent, while I screamed. Someone, I don't remember who, jumped to his rescue. I thought I had almost lost him, which Jack, of course, denied, claiming he was just having fun.

A special honor occurred when Jack was elected president of the St. Louis Council on World Affairs, an organization that brought national and world leaders to the community. It was a thrilling time with numerous lectures and social evenings, always a tuxedo and formal dress event. Two unforgettable speakers were Secretary of State Henry Kissinger and Ambassador Orofino from Argentina. At the banquet honoring Dr. Kissinger, Jack hosted Nancy Kissinger, while I was honored to be Dr. Kissinger's dinner partner, on the opposite side of the dais.

Nancy Kissinger, John Anthony Brown, and Dr. Henry Kissinger, Secretary of State, when he spoke before the St. Louis Council on World Affairs.
Photograph, courtesy of the St. Louis Globe-Democrat

The Kissingers were quite distinctive in their appearance. While he was short and stocky with dark penetrating eyes, Nancy was tall--over six feet--and unusually thin, accentuated by her ankle-length black dress. The four of us had something in common; they were also newlyweds in 1974, and Nancy was twenty years, or more, younger than her husband. I recall that Dr. Kissinger's German accent was sometimes difficult to understand, but, without a doubt, he is the most intelligent person I have ever been privileged to host as my dinner guest.

While Dr. Kissinger was very serious in his demeanor, Ambassador Orofino was, perhaps, the most charming South American I have ever encountered. Tall and rather portly, Mr. Orofino had luminous eyes and knew how to flatter a woman. The evening we picked the Ambassador up at his hotel, I rode with him in the backseat, while Jack sat in the passenger seat next to our driver. Jack was absolutely flabbergasted at my animated conversation with our guest. I don't remember the exact content of our exchange, but I do know the Ambassador made me feel special, which I have never forgotten.

During this period, we also suffered heartache with Jack's youngest son, David. We were having dinner when the telephone rang. The call was from the police. David was in the St. Charles County jail. He and a friend had been arrested for growing and selling marijuana. Leaving dinner unfinished, Jack jumped into his car and was off to bail David out of jail. How much was the bail? Whatever the amount, it was more than we had to spare.

Several hours later, Jack returned, bringing a bearded David with him. What a forlorn-looking, embarrassed young man he was. Jack may have had some thoughts about David's living with us, but that might have upset the atmosphere we were trying to create for Bill. Furthermore, I was sure that David had no interest whatsoever in living with us at that time.

On the other hand, David and I had become friends when he was a student at Lindenwood. Long before his dad and I fell in love, David often came to my office just to chat. Difficult as it was not to pass judgment on his lifestyle, I was committed to be his listening friend, not his stepmother. David was in and out of our home for several weeks, and he eventually moved to Fulton, Missouri, where he met Katie, the love of his life. Eventually, they both came to live with us in Ohio.

During this stressful scenario, Jack was in the midst of establishing a consulting business. He had numerous connections, including the Danforth Foundation, the Ford Foundation, and the U.S. Office of Education. Contracts were cemented with all three agencies. For two years, Jack traveled fifteen days a month to numerous colleges across the country. I scheduled his meetings, made his airplane reservations, and took care of the office.

We had converted a corner bedroom into a delightful work space with a perfect view of the quiet tree-lined neighborhood. The morning sun streamed in the southeast window, and the afternoon sun cast its glow through the floor-to-ceiling west window. It was before the days of computers, so I typed correspondence and reports on an electric Smith-Corona typewriter.

A born teacher and writer, Jack had been a journalist and editor before becoming a college administrator. He dictated his reports on a small transcriber he carried with him when he visited colleges. His narratives were more like essays than a factual account. I soaked up all the knowledge my brain could hold, and became a much better writer.

In addition to my improved writing skills, one of the most important attributes about this period of my life is that I was home when Bill arrived from school. In the mornings, if he was running late or didn't want to ride his bicycle, I was also available to drive him to school.

On Saturdays at 5 a.m., before the sun was up, I car-pooled with several other mothers as we alternated driving our sons to tennis lessons. When it was my time to drive, I usually dozed in my car or read a mystery novel while the boys batted the ball across the net.

Treasured times were also spent reading, gardening, and playing bridge with life-long friends. While I have special memories of my St. Louis bridge-playing buddies, I found myself knee-deep in Jack's consulting business. I eventually did some consulting of my own, so there was little time for bridge or to see friends.

This is the period when I also was planning, developing, and testing new outpatient procedures for the radiology department at St. Luke's Hospital. My hours were flexible and I worked short days, so it didn't infringe upon my work with Jack, or our travel and vacation plans.

The second summer of our marriage, we returned to Maine. In order to take family and pets with us, we needed a large automobile. We sold the Oldsmobile and my Volkswagen bug, and purchased an International Harvester van. Five of us made the trip: Jack; his twenty-five-year-old daughter, Barbara; Bill and his friend, Eric; Sandy, the collie; and me. Patrick stayed with Bill's dad, and a neighbor looked after Charlie. While Barbara had been less than enthusiastic about her dad's new marriage, she wanted to spend time with him, and probably wanted to check me over as well.

The Maine trip was an exciting adventure for blond, blue-eyed Eric, who had never journeyed beyond Missouri's borders. A quiet, well-behaved thirteen-year-old, Eric was a perfect travel buddy for Bill. Jack, Barbara, and I shared the driving. We arrived at our cabin late in the morning on the second day after driving thirteen hundred miles. We were exhausted, but there was no time for sleep.

Boards had to be removed from windows, dead mice swept from floors, furniture dusted, and, above all, the bathroom cleaned. Ventilation was crucial, and disinfectant a must. Each person was assigned a task and, by mid-afternoon, the place was livable.

Jack and I purchased fixings for dinner at the Fayette Country Store, while the boys were off to swim and fish, with Barbara and Sandy as life guards. For two weeks, we swam, boated, fished, watched the moon come up, counted the stars, and played Checkers, Hearts, and Monopoly. Mosquitoes were rampant, but we ignored them. Bill and Eric explored every nook and cranny of the shoreline.

Toward the end of our stay, Jack and I left Barbara with the boys, and flew to Alfred University in upstate New York, where Jack was a candidate for the presidency. We were treated royally, but it was not the place for us. Like shopping for a new dress, you know it when you see it.

When we returned to the cabin we found that Sandy had tangled with a porcupine, who'd imbedded dozens of quills in the collie's nose. Barbara, Bill, and Eric wrapped her in a blanket and drove our van over dark country roads, searching for an animal hospital. Long past midnight, they spotted a sign: "Veterinarian." The house was dark, but they knocked anyway, and were admitted by a sleepy-eyed elderly man.

Barbara and the boys held Sandy on the table, while the vet removed the quills from the dog's nose with a heavy-duty pair of pliers. Poor Sandy; she had never seen one of those prickly creatures before, nor would she want to again. Several days later, we left for home.

That fall and the following winter, Jack's consulting business grew beyond all expectations. He thoroughly enjoyed working with foundation leaders, and observing the national education scene. It allowed him to perceive situations and make recommendations without becoming emotionally involved.

While I missed Jack when he traveled, I knew he was happy and his health had improved immensely. He would arrive home from his travels with reams of yellow legal pads and dictating tapes. I had difficulty keeping up with all the reports, but I enjoyed learning about the different organizational styles of the various colleges and universities.

Our lives brimmed with work, family, and friends. Beginning our second year of marriage, we hosted a family reunion with my mother's siblings and numerous first cousins. From a small family himself, Jack was delighted to have acquired new relatives. As if he was a mannequin in a department store window, like it or not, he was on display with my numerous aunts, uncles, and cousins. Little did we know that our lives would soon be on continual exhibit.

The experience at Alfred University had intensified Jack's dream of a college presidency, but as the consulting business grew, such thoughts had been moved to the back burner.

One day in early summer, the phone rang. On the other end of the line was the chairman of the board of Muskingum College in New Concord, Ohio. Introducing himself as Philip Caldwell, also president of The Ford Motor Company, he said, "Would you consider being a candidate for the presidency of Muskingum College?" Jack knew of Muskingum, but it was a new word in my vocabulary.

Located in the rolling hills of southeastern Ohio, in a tiny town of two thousand people, the private college with fewer than one thousand students was committed to liberal arts education. After Jack's lengthy discussion with Mr. Caldwell, which was followed by our own deliberations, we accepted his invitation to visit the campus.

Two days later, Jack and I flew to Columbus and were met by Mr. Caldwell, a warm, personable man, probably in his mid-fifties, with not a wrinkle or gray hair to be seen. We rode in his blue-gray Lincoln Town Car to New Concord.

Built on three hills that surrounded a lake, a gazebo, and a football stadium in the valley, the campus was a picturesque scene with its brick buildings, red-tiled roofs, and tree-lined streets. After touring the campus and meeting with trustees, faculty, administrators, and students, we were impressed. They had piqued our interest.

As if we had come home, we felt warmth, synergy, and connection with the people, unlike any other experience. At the end of the day, having a few moments of privacy, Jack and I concluded that Muskingum would be the ideal place for us to return to academia. We were excited about the prospect, but we tempered our enthusiasm. We wanted to take Bill for a visit before making a decision. After all, it would be his home, too.

The morning after returning to St. Louis, we made arrangements with Mr. Caldwell to visit Muskingum again the following week. While fifteen-year-old Bill was not remotely interested in moving anywhere, he was happy to miss two days of school. He agreed to accompany us to Ohio.

We toured the campus again, as well as the surrounding community, but most of my time was spent with Bill at John Glenn High School, where we talked with students, teachers, and coaches. Bill seemed to like the school, the people he met, and the athletic program offerings.

Most importantly, we made a thorough inspection of the president's house, which had stood vacant for several years. Like an empty castle, the place was enormous and sparsely furnished. Bill could have played basketball in the living room. The upstairs had four bedrooms and three baths. Bill had his own bathroom as well as his own private staircase leading to the kitchen. That thought rather pleased him. The kitchen had a cozy booth, a panoramic view of the campus, and more cabinets and counter space than I had ever experienced. Other than needing a little paint, the kitchen was a joy to behold.

At the end of the day, we said our farewells, but, instinctively, Jack and I knew Muskingum College was to be our new home. Jack had been offered the presidency, and I was excited to share the opportunity with him. He had told Mr. Caldwell about his health history and that he could not accept the presidency without a complete physical examination and approval by his cardiologist. Upon our return to St. Louis, Jack was admitted to St. Luke's Hospital for three days of tests. I'll never forget Dr. Rainey's parting words, "Go give'em hell."

We were expected in New Concord for the beginning of the fall term, and we were in a tailspin with only three weeks to go. We hustled to make moving arrangements, packed what seemed like hundreds of boxes, and tended to thousands of details. All of these activities slowly and painfully disconnected us from a city, a neighborhood, and a home we had come to love.

We were also leaving Bill's dad, his grandparents, and my mom and dad behind. In addition, Bill was saying goodbye to friends he had known all his young life. Needless to say, Bill was less than joyous, and parting was tough.

As the moving van pulled away on August 15, Jack, Bill, our three pets, and I piled into our new silver Ford Granada. We were packed like sardines in a can and knew instantly that selling our van had been a mistake. It was an adventuresome trip, to say the least.

Jack drove and Bill sat in the navigator's seat with Patrick on the floor between his legs. We rotated the driving, but most of the time I shared the back seat with the collie, and Charlie curled up on the back window ledge. She looked like a miniature panther and hollered like a banshee most of the trip. Years later, and before she died at the age of nineteen, Charlie's voice would find a new level as she howled to the sounds of music, particularly the French horn.

Staying overnight in a motel with our animals was out of the question. In the early morning hours, we pulled into a rest area, turned off the lights, and slept a few hours. Sleep was sporadic, and one or the other of us was constantly walking one of the pets. Arriving in New Concord after ten hours, and with little sleep, alas, we found the moving van awaiting our arrival.

Thus, the last chapter of our exhilarating odyssey began.

After the move and once we were settled, Bill flew to St. Louis for a week's visit with his dad and grandparents. I had faith he would eventually love life in the rural southern Ohio community. And that he did.

Five days after returning from his trip to Missouri, Bill kicked a fifty-yard punt in his first football game for John Glenn High School. It seemed the entire town turned out for the game, and the roar of the crowd in St. Clairsville, Ohio was unbelievable. The next year Bill gave up football and became a star forward on the John Glenn basketball team. Years later, he married Christina Miller, a high school classmate and Muskingum College graduate. Christy was a freshman during our last year at the college.

For three-and-a-half years, our lives intertwined with students, faculty, trustees, and alumni. Every day brimmed with plans, ideas, dreams, events, and alumni gatherings from Fort Lauderdale to San Francisco. The most memorable experiences were intimate suppers with students around a cozy fire in our home, or in one of the fraternity houses; small staff luncheons, which I personally prepared; and dinners with faculty and trustees. These were the special people, hours, and conversations we would never forget. Years later, from time to time, I have encountered former students on the streets of Columbus. They remember as if it were yesterday.

And our friend, Garrison Howard, also would remember, for he served on the Muskingum College Board of Trustees for three years after Jack died.

When Garrison learned the shattering news, he planned to be on the next flight to St. Louis. I regretted telling him that Jack's doctor discouraged visitors. I promised to keep him informed. "Please tell Jack I love him, and you, too," he said.

In addition to the numerous phone conversations with family and friends, letters and cards also began to arrive. The first came from Muskingum's basketball team; another from our dear friends, Nora and Rob Abrams; and, the last in the stack on that day was a card from the All Around Club, a literary organization in Zanesville that I had been invited to join. Requirements for membership included the annual presentation of a paper on a topic of personal interest.

Since we were in the process of completing our retreat cottage, I chose Williamsburg architecture for my first paper. It was fortunate that I had the following spring and summer to do my research before presenting in the fall. How considerate it was of the club members to send Jack a card, I thought. The cards and phone calls continued to multiply, as did my hospital friends.

One of those friends was a young intern named Michael Trenor, a student at St. Louis University Medical School who served his internship at St. Luke's. Michael had been on duty our first night at the hospital. He had become very fond of Jack, and was in constant vigil, praying for his survival. Late one evening, he stopped to share a picture of his proudest possession, his nine-month-old daughter, Kim. It was long past time for him to head home, so after a short visit, we said goodnight. I was glad to see Michael, but I was weary.

Shortly thereafter, Jack was sleeping and so was my roommate, another snoring bedfellow. I curled up with my pillow and blanket on one of the overstuffed chairs, turned off the lights, except for my reading lamp, and wrote in my journal.

Journal writing had entered my life quite by accident. A physician, who had been on duty the night of our arrival, stopped me one afternoon as I wandered the corridor, and asked if we could talk. Originally from India, Dr. Ganga was quite striking with his glistening bronze skin and black hair against his white hospital garb. We stepped into a small waiting area off the main corridor. Except for two upholstered love seats, an attractive end table and a lamp, the room was empty. The warm light flowing from the single lamp provided an inviting atmosphere.

Although Dr. Ganga was no longer on duty in the ICU, much to my surprise he had been checking on Jack every day. He commended me for staying in the hospital, and proceeded to tell me that when a person is hospitalized in India, a family member must stay with the patient twenty-four hours a day. The family is important to the patient's well being, it is helpful for the family or spouse to know what is happening, and the family also can be of assistance to the medical staff, if needed.

Dr. Ganga had been in America for five years, and St. Luke's was his third teaching hospital. I was the first non-patient he had observed living in the hospital. What a humbling experience it was when Dr. Ganga praised me for restoring his faith in the American people. I explained to him that, in America, families are not normally encouraged to spend the night in the hospital, particularly in intensive care.

Today, some hospital units have separate rooms where families may stay, but it is not normally sanctioned in intensive care units, where time with a patient is usually limited to five or ten minutes every hour. I told Dr. Ganga that I was quite surprised, but pleased, when Dr. Rainey insisted I stay in the ICU. I could never have left Jack alone. Before we parted, I thanked Dr. Ganga for his generous compliment, and for inspiring me to think about the unusual experience I was having.

After saying farewell to Dr. Ganga, I immediately went to my locker and retrieved my favorite writing tools, two pencils and a yellow legal pad. From that time on, writing occupied late evening hours for the remainder of my hospital stay.

Writing until after two o'clock and before drifting off to sleep, I glanced at the light coming in the six-foot window overlooking the courtyard below. Snowflakes were gently falling, and the reflection from the full moon cast shimmering icicles on the window; a beautiful site in the stillness of the night.

How I longed for the great outdoors of the farm, where I could breathe fresh air and Jack's withered body could heal. I prayed for Jack's recovery, and wondered when spring would come. As I floated off to sleep, I wondered where we would be when the earth turned green. Only God could answer that question.

Day 10

Waking with a start the next morning, I was surprised to hear voices and see briskly moving traffic in the hallway. I couldn't believe it. I had slept for nine hours without interruption, and with no dreams I could recollect. I raced to Jack's room, thinking he would be awake, only to find him snoring. I checked all the monitors and hanging bottles. Much to my relief, his heart rate had slowed to 104. Filled with gratitude, I was off to freshen up and enjoy my new morning routine in the coffee shop with the *St. Louis Globe Democrat*.

Rested and encouraged, I treated myself to grapefruit, poached eggs on whole wheat toast, two slices of bacon, and, of course, coffee. Radiology technician Antonio Frapo, stopped by to say hello and inquire about Jack. Antonio was from Greece; a tall, muscular man, he had a ruddy complexion, reddish brown hair, and sapphire eyes that complemented his blue uniform. We chatted briefly about scheduling procedures, which I had helped to organize several years previous.

Our paths would continue to cross from time to time in the hospital corridor. Antonio always asked about Jack, and expressed amazement at my stamina. I continued to be impressed with the wealth of care-giving demonstrated by the hospital staff.

I finished my breakfast and hurried to Jack's room to find him still asleep. Stella, one of the LPN's, said he had been awake only briefly. Stella was another one of the nurses Jack had written about in his newspaper column:

> "...I think of the nurse who changed the linens on my bed four times, three nights running, without a murmur of complaint. She responded to my apology, for the nuisance I was causing her, by saying, "Don't you fail to call me if you need your linen changed a fifth time. It won't do you any good lying here in a cold sweat..."

Stella wore her heart on her sleeve, and put her patient's well-being in the forefront of her work. As I left the room, I asked her to tell Jack I had gone to see Maria and would return shortly.

Although I found Maria in excruciating pain, she looked stunning in her colorful sarong of yellow, red, blue, and shades of purple. She was scheduled for surgery, but the date had not been decided. For now, she was in traction to reduce the possibility of motion and further pain. As always, Maria expressed a great deal of emotion about Jack, and little concern about her own health. Before her spinal problems developed, she had planned to make a trip to her home in Burma.

The eldest of nine children, Maria talked about home with a sense of fear and hesitancy. Her father had died three months after Maria had come to the United States, and she had not seen her mother since. Her mother was not alone; three of her sons and their families lived with her, but Maria missed her mother. She was fearful that traveling to see her mother would not take place anytime soon. When Maria's lunch arrived, I departed, promising to return later in the day.

Upon my return to the ICU, I found Jack still snoring. Shortly, he woke, albeit briefly, to ask, "Is Nancy all right?" Dr. Rainey stopped in to remove the Lidocaine, a drug that slowed the heart rate, and he said Jack should be more alert in a few hours. He expressed concern about the continuing atrial fibrillation, but, on the other hand, he said Jack might have to live with that irregularity forever. If he lives, I thought, we will deal with whatever is necessary.

After Dr. Rainey left, and while Jack was still sleeping, I escaped to the coffee shop to have a special treat. A life-long lover of chocolate, particularly dark chocolate, I allowed myself a hot fudge sundae, no nuts, cherries or whipped cream; just ice cream and chocolate. As it slithered down my throat, each spoonful fed my chocolate craving. Savoring every mouthful, I made it last as long as possible. Since I seemed to be losing weight, maybe I could have another. But I didn't. Still, it was a simple pleasure and one that gave me great enjoyment at a time when such treats were lacking in my life.

I continued with my journal writing. More and more I gained strength from writing, meditating, and thinking alone. When I wasn't praying or keeping my mind occupied, I worried. When I stewed, my thoughts became cloudy and cluttered. The only way to clear the cobwebs was to pick up a pencil and start writing. Being a practical person by nature, I was determined to face reality, whatever it might be.

Life or death, I had to somehow be prepared to face the future and to concentrate on Jack getting well. Thinking positively better enabled me to provide the strength and love that Jack needed for survival. I firmly believed that faith, hope, and love would make the difference.

Rejuvenated after my chocolate infusion, I returned to Jack's room to find him awake and incredibly alert. Water, water, and more water was all he wanted. He had experienced no water or food for an entire week. What fluid had entered his body had been removed by dialysis. Becoming more alert with each sip, Jack slowly began to realize where he was, and that he had been in the hospital for a very long time. Weak as he was, suddenly, in a very demanding voice, he said, "Get me out of here."

It took hours of persuasive talking to convince him why it was not possible for him to leave the hospital. I suggested we should find out what Dr. Rainey's plans were for moving him to another room. What a pipe dream, I thought. Not knowing whether a different room was possible, I prayed he could be moved out of intensive care soon. It was such a claustrophobic environment.

Since Jack had not slept much during the previous week, he had a lot of catching up to do. Sitting by his bed, I read most of the afternoon and evening while he appeared to be in a restful sleep. It was such a deep sleep that the nurse and I had a hard time waking him for supper. His first meal consisted of chicken broth and strawberry Jell-o. He enjoyed the Jell-o, but the chicken broth, with no seasonings, was very displeasing. He pushed it away and returned to sleep.

Later, a group of student nurses invited me to join them for a spaghetti dinner in the hospital cafeteria. It wasn't the best pasta I had ever eaten, but it was another one of life's little pleasures. Soul food for times of trouble, and joyful conversation with young people brightened my spirits.

One of the great benefits Jack and I enjoyed in our work with small colleges was the satisfaction that comes from connecting with young people. Through laughter and joy, on that night, the student nurses lightened my load, if only for a brief moment.

The remainder of the evening was quiet for me, but not for the ICU nurses. Sylvia wasn't working that evening and, though she certainly deserved a night off, I missed her when she wasn't there. She had a wonderful way of elevating Jack's spirits, so easily depressed. There were only one R.N. and three LPNs, including Stella, on duty that night. They had more than they could handle. Stella kept saying, "Oh my God, oh my God."

A two-hundred-ninety-pound man with a pacemaker had ventricular tachycardia, a very rapid heart beat. Another patient who had just arrived was so upset she wouldn't take her clothes off. If she had anything to say about it, no one else was going to disrobe her either. Jack slept through it all.

I listened to the commotion as long as I could stand it and then returned several phone messages. I had a wonderful chat with David; a call to a college classmate and horseback riding instructor at Lindenwood; and a special call to Joe Myers, the chairman of Muskingum's board of trustees. Joe and his wife had become close friends. The previous summer, they had surprised us with a food processor, new on the market at the time. To this day, I use the same processor with all the original blades. Their generosity had overwhelmed us. As I sat in the cramped phone booth, Joe said "Give my love to Jack, but save some for you."

Before calling it a day, I dialed Bill. He sounded lonely, tired, and cantankerous, just like Jack. My son obviously needed his mother and some good old-fashioned TLC. I thought that if Jack continued to improve, maybe I could go home for a few days. I was torn between my priorities and the two most important people in my life.

Some phone conversations cheered my spirits and others were sad, but they were my life-line and I held on tight to every caller. I needed to know they were there for me, and that I was there for them.

Later in the evening, I wrote in my journal: "I pray Jack makes it. He is so fragile, but still his vital signs are good. It's tough, God, but I'm hanging in there. It's so easy to worry and fear the future. I pray that I will have enough courage and stamina to get us through the next several months."

Day 11

About six o'clock the next morning, one of the nurses woke me to say that Jack was asking for me. Evidently, he had been awake half the night, coughing up sputum from his lungs, a good sign.

His first words to me were, "Where in the hell have you been the last three days?" I was startled; however, I believed it was an indication that he was getting better. Dr. Rainey stopped in a short time later and said, "He is much better this morning." Jack responded, "That's a lot of propaganda."

It was a very confusing day for him. One minute, he was in California, the next, in Maine. If I went anywhere out of his sight, he became angry. As he became more and more alert, many happenings–annoying to me all along–began to bother Jack as well. An example was the constant chatter of voices at the nurses' station. I was told that it is an on-going problem in ICUs everywhere. I hoped they would move Jack to one of the more isolated, quieter rooms.

"A miserable experience," Jack said one evening. Oh, if he only had known what horror he had been through. "Don't leave me; help me get solid again," he pleaded from the depths of his soul. As I watched him suffer, it pained my heart to its deepest crevice. I left him only to eat or go to the bathroom. Sitting with Jack, day in and day out, I began to read a book one of the doctors had lent me about the psycho-social aspects of cardiac care. It was extremely technical and raised more questions than it did answers. For example, did the toxicity to Digoxin cause the return of Jack's extra heartbeats, or were the additional beats a result of congestive heart failure? It was one of many questions that I would ask Dr. Rainey the next day.

Chapter V

A LITTLE MIRACLE

Day 12

    With the dawning of Monday, January 26, Jack was beginning to look like his old self. For the first time, I felt optimistic. The gray pallor slowly had been replaced with a hint of color, and his eyes seemed to come to life as if they had been in deep slumber, which, of course, they had. Upon removal of the intravenous tubes and the urinary catheter, he had freedom of motion for the first time in ten days. A physical therapist appeared to begin Jack's exercise program. After a head wash and real food, Jack exclaimed that he felt like a new man and, as promised, the nurses moved his bed to a quiet corner of the ICU.

    Miracle of miracles, the day was an incredible new beginning. I could hardly believe the sudden turn of events.

    Later, Jack inquired, "What happened to me today?" Evidently the process of moving had stimulated his brain cells. Out of the blue, and much to my surprise, he asked about David, Katie, Bill, and his new granddaughter, Anthony's first child. Maybe, I thought, he is finally going to reenter the world, and is ready to hear news of family and friends.

    That afternoon, I discovered that someone had taken four or five messages for me in 'my' phone booth; names and numbers were scribbled on a slip of paper and taped to the telephone. One of the calls was from the Abrams in New Concord. They wanted to know how Jack was doing, and inquired if they could do anything for me. I was at a loss for words; their love, prayers, and friendship were all I needed at that moment. Although I was lonely beyond words, never have I felt such incredible support from so many friends, as well as people I barely knew.

    Suddenly, the ring of the telephone startled me. The person on the other end was Jack's longtime friend, Peter Merrimon.

I *first met Peter when Jack and I traveled to Washington early in our*

relationship. Most often, we stayed at Peter's home and always looked forward to his dinner parties. Situated in northwest Washington, his comfortable two-story bungalow was tastefully decorated. Most of the furnishings were contemporary Scandinavian birch, with a color scheme of blues and whites, reflecting his love of the sea. Peter's home-away-from-home was a twenty-four-foot sailboat.

Not only were the food and wine exceptional at Peter's soirees, but the invigorating conversation was usually animated with the latest happenings in the Capitol. Sometimes, the occasion was a stand-up cocktail buffet, with guests from a variety of countries. Other times, the affair was an intimate dinner for six or eight friends. It was forever interesting to see who the other guests might be.

Peter's women friends always added an intriguing element to any evening. The variety of styles and personalities simply amazed me. One of my favorites was Liz, a state department colleague in her late forties. An earth-mother type, Liz loved to cook, and grew plants in abundance on the balcony of her apartment. Another friend, Rosie, quietly came and softly left, as if she were an angel floating about, seldom if ever uttering a word. Rosie was thirty years younger than Peter and a student at American University. Angelina, also a student, was a joyful, wispy gal from Rumania, perhaps the daughter Peter never had. Then, there was Michelle, a career diplomat from France, who loved the arts, and was an excellent chef. On rare occasions she would join us for dinner and the theater.

Although Michelle seemed more Peter's style, Jack and I enjoyed Liz as well and, of course, Peter loved all of his women. Although we were continually mystified by their comings and goings, they certainly provided excitement to Peter's life.

Then, there was Peter's passion for the sea. I'll never forget the summer that Jack and I married. To celebrate the occasion, Peter invited us to join him for a week of sailing off the coast of Maine. After four weeks of marital togetherness at our cabin, we were ready for adventure. We agreed to meet at eleven o'clock on a Monday at Pier III, Rockland, Maine.

There was no speedy way from our cabin on Lake Echo to Rockland, so we opted to enjoy the back country roads. The drive was spectacular. There were shimmering crystal clear lakes with ducks, geese, and loons sunning themselves on the banks, summer cottages dotted the shorelines amidst tall, majestic pine trees, and wild flowers of every kind and color, as if God's paint brush had just swept the landscape.

As we approached Rockland, the landscape shifted dramatically, as the mountainous and rocky coastline rose in the distance. Located on Penobscot Bay, Rockland today has a population of approximately eight thousand people. Historically, the main industry has been ship building, rock quarrying, lobsters, and commercial fishing. The Wyeth Center is also a major attraction in Rockland, housing many of the original drawings of Andrew Wyeth. Jack and I planned to visit the museum later that summer.

Promptly at eleven o'clock, we met Peter at his boat, The Owl and the Pussycat, so christened by his former wife. A few years older than Jack, Peter was a distinguished-looking man with dark eyes, snow-white hair, and a ruddy, weathered complexion. Carrying himself with a straight posture on his five-foot eleven-inch frame, he kept himself trim, in spite of his Washington social calendar. On several trips to Washington, Jack and I had sailed on the Chesapeake with Peter and one or more of his female friends. As we prepared to sail on the Atlantic that morning, I was pleased there were only the three of us.

Like the three musketeers, we were off to the nearest grocer. The twenty-four-foot boat was ready to cruise, but Peter had awaited our arrival before purchasing food. Our shopping consisted of the basics for breakfast and lunch–fresh berries, cereal, blueberry muffins, lunch meats, tomatoes, lettuce, and a few snacks for the cocktail hour, faithfully observed by our host at five o'clock sharp, on land or sea. Most evenings, we planned to go ashore for dinner.

The sun was shining on our day with an azure blue sky, no clouds, and a perfect wind for sailing. I was in heaven except for one apprehension. How was I going to survive five days stranded on a sailboat with nowhere to escape, but overboard? It would not be easy. When we were traversing rough waters or high winds, with Jack and Peter yelling back and forth to each other, one steered the rudder and the other steadied the sails. I was usually below deck holding on for dear life, probably with my head undercover or buried in a book.

Having a life-long love affair with books, I loved to read a good murder mystery in the bathroom–still do. The head, as it is called in the boating world, was so tiny that you couldn't turn around, much less read a book. Tricks for getting in and out of the toilet included leaving one foot in the corridor while sliding your rear end onto the seat, then lifting your knees together, along with both feet and swinging them over the threshold, and finally closing the door. What an ordeal! Even if you didn't have claustrophobia, the head was no place for reading. Moreover, taking a shower was not worth the torment, when the Atlantic Ocean was right out the front door.

Below deck in the stern was the master bedroom, with its own privacy door, which Peter had reserved for our stay. We were grateful, as it was the only place Jack and I could be alone. After all, we were newlyweds and savored our privacy. Once or twice, we disappeared in the middle of the day to read or nap after lunch. Although Peter had many women friends, I came to realize that he was jealous of Jack's and my relationship. He often asked, "Don't you have a twin sister somewhere?" I was flattered.

Born in Maine and educated in private schools, Peter was an only child. By the time he and Jack became friends, his parents were deceased, and two wives had divorced him. Although Peter could be a generous and loving man when he wanted to, he also could be overbearing. There were times during our five-day journey that I wanted to turn and run the other way, but there was nowhere to hide.

All that being said, Peter was an expert sailor, a good cook, and an excellent host as well. What more could a woman want than to be wined and dined on a secluded sailboat for five days with two intelligent, attractive men?

We laughed a lot and our conversations covered every conceivable topic imaginable, ranging from what Jack was going to do about his troublesome faculty, to the best way to cook lobster, to our childhoods and our children, to how to avoid becoming seasick, to how Washington politicians were going to navigate our relationship with other countries, mainly Russia. Never could we have dreamt that, years later, President Reagan would end our Cold War with Russia.

While Jack and I were Republicans, Peter was a staunch Democrat. With President Nixon in the White House in 1973, and Gerald Ford the newly appointed vice-president, there was a good deal of laughter as well as friendly discord as we sailed the north Atlantic.

The only real animosity of the week was caused by the weather, mainly rough waters as we sailed towards Bar Harbor and then Nova Scotia. On one occasion, with the likelihood we might not be able to go ashore for dinner, we docked at the furthermost northern peninsula of Bar Harbor to purchase fresh seafood for lunch and steaks for dinner. As we returned to the boat, a storm approached in the distance. Slowly and quietly, the ocean began to churn.

Trying to ignore the treacherous conditions, Peter did his best to guide the rudder through the rising and ebbing of the waves while Jack went to the galley below to prepare a fresh crab and shrimp salad for lunch.

Jack nibbled as he worked–cutting up seafood, celery, and spring onions. Suddenly, he let go of the chopping knife and ran for the head. Yes, he was seasick. Although Peter and I sympathized with his agony, we nevertheless enjoyed his gourmet creation while he lay in misery.

After the turbulent waters had subsided, we dropped anchor in a secluded cove. It was my time for kitchen duty. I created a Caesar salad with fresh parmesan and garlic croutons, while topside, Jack and Peter cooked T-bone steaks on a portable grill. Jack was ravenous and anxious to enjoy a glass of cabernet sauvignon with his steak. Obviously, he had recovered.

It was a beautiful, full-moon evening with trillions of stars blinking in the heavens. After dinner, we took turns with the binoculars, searching for the big and small dippers, the Milky Way, Venus, and Mars. Later, as the gentle waters flowed and the moon's reflection streamed through our porthole, Jack and I fell asleep, locked in each other's arms.

The week was unforgettable, and one of the most pleasant excursions we ever shared with Peter. When we docked at Rockland on Friday morning, we were glad to shed our sea shoes and to feel Mother Earth under foot again. Although we had enjoyed Peter's generous hospitality, we were excited to return to our cabin in the woods.

I thought about those glorious five days when I heard Peter's voice that evening at the hospital. He was calling from Washington, but probably would have preferred to be snowbound with his friends in New Concord. Peter was calling to see how his buddy was progressing. I detected an uneasy agitation in his tone and knew something was bothering him.

The previous year, Jack had hired Peter as a consultant to the college's public relations office. After ten months, Jack and the senior staff concluded that, while Peter had provided outstanding leadership, his services were no longer necessary. I would eventually learn that Peter was not overjoyed with this decision.

Peter had rented an apartment in the village, immersed himself in the life of the college, made new friends, including an attractive gal on the admissions staff, and also loved sharing evenings with our family.

Conversations around the dinner table were spirited, interesting, and always educational. David particularly loved to play the devil's advocate with his dad and Peter, immensely enjoying their repartee. Unfortunately and regrettably, Peter would occasionally presume to tell Jack how to run the college—much to my consternation. Jack, always the diplomat, usually took the commentary in stride. This intrusion not only bothered me, but I felt that Jack's territory was being trespassed. Thus, when Jack became ill, I shielded our private time like a Swiss Pontifical Guard.

Once again, Peter was reaching out to us. Out of the blue and much to my shock, Peter asked me whose idea it was that he not return to the campus after the Christmas holidays. Without a moment's hesitation, I replied, "It was a joint decision of the administration." I don't think he believed me.

In light of Jack's critical situation, the audacity of Peter to corner me on the subject was beyond my comprehension. With as much grace as I could muster, I quietly thanked Peter for his call, said goodnight, and told him I would be in touch when Jack's health improved.

By the time I returned to Jack, I wore a smile from ear to ear. Jack and I shared everything, so it was difficult to tell a little "white lie." There was no way I could share the gist of my conversation with Peter. I only hoped Jack's intuitive mind could not read my thoughts, and I prayed that God would forgive me for my sin of omission.

Day 13

After a restless night, a new day dawned and there were more important things to worry about. Whatever I did to try and elevate Jack's spirits; he was in a profound state of confusion. As if he were an eagle in the sky, one minute he was in Ohio, the next in California, Maine, Washington, or St. Louis. Then, to my grave concern, another crisis appeared on the horizon.

Jack's eyes had turned pea-green, the alarm bell for malfunctioning of the liver. His body seemed to be in a volatile state and his spirit was soaring around, causing damage here and there, like a tornado. I wondered what the day would bring. My aunt and uncle had invited me to dinner. Did I dare think I might be able to go? Fortunately, by evening Jack's condition was on a more stable footing.

After assuring him that the night nurse had my uncle's phone number, I kissed Jack goodnight and left the hospital for my first excursion in twelve days. The cold winter air felt like a touch of heaven as it lightly brushed my skin and filled my starving lungs. I walked down the hospital steps to my parents' waiting car, suddenly exhilarated by the rush of fresh oxygen in my veins. I like to think it was God's energy.

Although I was excited to have an evening out, I also was apprehensive because I would be expected to carry on a social conversation. Locked in my protective shell, I didn't want to communicate with anyone. Thinking back, it was almost as if I had forgotten how to carry on a conversation.

Herman, my dad's brother, and his wife, Daphne, lived in a small bungalow on a narrow dead-end street in the southern part of the city. Tall and lanky with jet black hair, Herman excelled in management with Union Electric for more than thirty years. A house wife and proud of it, Daphne was a great cook. She had a beautiful complexion, sparkling brown eyes, and sandy brown hair. Her style and demeanor always made me think of Edith Bunker in "All in the Family."

Herman and Daphne raised three boys, each with their own distinct personalities. The youngest son was diverse in his occupations as a university professor, author of numerous romance novels, and a day-trader in the stock market; the middle son served in the military and worked for the postal service; and, the eldest son was a manager with a national retail store.

None of the boys married, and two lived at home most of their lives. After many years of psychological problems, the middle son committed suicide. Only George, the eldest son, joined us for dinner that evening.

The gathering was motivated by my presence in St. Louis, as well as that of my Mississippi cousin, William Alvis Parks, and his wife, Charlsie. They had a way of showing up whenever there was a critical illness or funeral in the family. I was delighted to see them and knew that our time together would be filled with nostalgic stories, laughter, and southern charm. What a godsend, I thought—maybe I wouldn't have to talk after all.

Like his father before him, William Alvis–always called by his double name–could tell one funny story after another, laughing so hard at his own jokes that it was difficult to understand his stories. He was tall and thin, with dancing blue eyes, and reminded me of John F. Kennedy. His wife, Charlsie, was (and still is) a handsome woman with a radiant personality and an infectious laugh.

Together, they raised five children and fourteen grandchildren.

William Alvis, or Daddy William as his family called him, was a generous, loving father and grandfather. A committed spiritual man, he was one of the most compassionate, giving, and joyous human beings I have ever encountered. God was truly in his heart. When William Alvis died years later, one of his daughters shared a poignant story about her father. It seems whenever someone asked William Alvis how he was, his favorite response was "Like a rose." He was truly like a rose, always blooming and filled with joy.

Over a delicious roast beef dinner, the conversation turned to horses–my Arabian horse in foal, and William Alvis's three Morgan horses. I remember we discussed breeding one of his horses with my twelve-year-old mare.

Regrettably, as my life changed, I sold my Arabians. Twenty-three years later, when William Alvis Parks died, I finally got to see his beautiful Morgan horses, two black stallions, each with a white star on their forehead, and a chestnut mare. I always regretted that it took me so long to get to Mississippi. Life with its twists and turns often leads us on a different path, and sometimes we never return to our dreams. I shall never forget those hours with William Alvis and Charlsie. Their infectious joy took me out of myself for a few hours.

While the evening holds special memories, my mind was constantly thinking of Jack. Before dinner was over, I had butterflies in my stomach, twitching nerves, and I became anxious to return to the hospital. I lived in great fear that something might happen to Jack when I wasn't there.

When I returned to the hospital, Jack awoke startled, but seemed glad to see me. In a desperate voice, he said, "I can't live without you." The feeling was mutual, but I was just relieved that he was alright.

Unlike the confident, self-assured man I had grown to love, no one will ever know how insecure he was at that moment.

Shortly, Jack drifted off to sleep and I placed a quick call to Bill. When he didn't answer, I called David and Katie to find all three were having a late dinner together. I was worried about Bill. Since an injury to his thigh during basketball practice, he had been in significant pain. His basketball coach was fearful of a calcium deposit. That evening, Bill conveyed the sad news. A visit to the doctor had determined that he definitely had a calcium deposit.

What a crushing disappointment. He sat on the bench the rest of the season. It also squashed his chances to play college basketball. I was relieved that he was with David and Katie, but I felt lonely, estranged, and consumed with guilt.

Not wanting to end our conversation, I told Bill I loved him, and that I would be home as soon as Jack got better. I hesitantly said goodnight and laid the phone in its cradle. The flowing tears felt hot on my cheeks.

Returning to the waiting room, I found a new roommate sleeping on "my sofa." An elderly lady, she had stolen my bed, my pillow, and my blanket. Having no other choice, I curled up on one of the small divans; while adequate, it was not comfortable. I tossed and turned most of the night. As if a strong wind were whistling through the trees, the snoring from the far side of the room was constant. I wished that I had put a reserved sign on my bed. It took me forever to fall asleep, but when I did, it was a deep slumber.

Day 14

By the time I awoke, Jack had eaten his breakfast. He was in a cheerful mood, but also disoriented. Dr. Poole stopped by later in the morning. Poole had ordered the dialysis and had as much to do with saving Jack's life as anyone. That morning he said to Jack, "You are a little miracle." Later, Jack retorted privately to me, "He's a smart aleck." The only people Jack liked were Dr. Rainey and his nurse, Sylvia.

Rolling back my memory calendar, I regret, with all my heart that Jack had to endure the agony and torture of the respirator and the peritoneal dialysis treatments. But, no one had told me that he was going to die. Thus, I had every reason to believe that he was going to live.

Since it was long past breakfast, I left Jack in Brenda's care and hurried to the coffee shop for a quick breakfast, then to visit Maria, and have my shower. Much to my surprise, I found Maria in traction. The doctors were trying to solve her problem without surgery. She was depressed, frustrated, and restless to return to her work. While I showered, I decided to buy her some flowers to brighten her room, as well as her mood. As if a waterfall was cleansing every pore, I was exhilarated and refreshed by the stimulation of the shower.

Feeling on top of the world, I returned to Jack's room to

find his lunch had arrived. Much to my surprise, he was feeding himself. Lunch consisted of stewed chicken, mashed potatoes, peas, and canned pears, but was without seasoning. Jack ate every bite. Step by step, a little progress was made each day.

In late afternoon, Dr. Rainey took time from his busy schedule to have a long conversation with us. He seemed in disarray, preoccupied, and looked in need of sleep. The good news was that Jack's heart seemed to have stabilized. "The fire is out," said Rainey. However, he went on to say that, due to the jaundiced liver, Jack would lack energy for another week or so, and might be on edge emotionally as well.

Rainey indicated we would have a planning session the following week. I was in disbelief, barely believing what my ears had heard. I knew the doctor was hoping to lift Jack's spirits, but I remember thinking, "Isn't he being overly optimistic?" All of a sudden Jack appeared to relax, and I breathed a sigh of relief.

I truly believe our faith had pulled us through the terrible crisis. Like maybe, just maybe, Jack was going to get out of the hospital after all. Patience was my motto, but how wonderful it would be to take him home.

We shared dinner that evening for the first time since arriving at St. Luke's. When Jack's meal was served, to my surprise, there was a tray for me as well. Although we preferred candlelight, crystal, and china, we were together. Jack was on the road to recovery and nothing else mattered. The roast beef, albeit dry, boiled potatoes, green beans, and peaches were nutritious and filling, but without an ounce of flavor, except for the fruit.

We spent the rest of the evening watching television. It's doubtful I was concentrating, so I really don't remember what we watched; probably some of our favorites such as, "Mash", "Columbo", or "Murder She Wrote." It was just pure joy to be holding hands, and talking when Jack felt like it.

I steered clear of discussing what had happened to him. Most of our conversation had to do with his children, my phone calls, and what was going on at the college; nothing too heavy was my motto.

One evening, he asked, "Why hasn't David been to see me?" I knew that question would come—how guilty I felt. If the doctor had allowed it, David could have driven to St. Louis, but he could not afford a plane ticket, nor did we have the funds. With Jack's alimony payments, there wasn't much surplus for extras.

Fortunately, our house and Jack's car were provided by the college. Those perks were a real bonus, because, in 1978, Jack's salary as a college president was only thirty-five thousand dollars a year.

So, what was my response to Jack's inquiry about David? I simply said, "The doctor thought it would be best for you not to have any visitors until you are stronger." I went on to say that, "Driving eight hours through the snow storms across the Midwest would have been treacherous." Additionally, it was important for David not to experience any more breaks in his education. The latter Jack understood and accepted.

Day 15

Although Jack had a good night's sleep, the following morning, as Rainey had predicted, I found him in a state of hopelessness and unusually nervous. He was trying to come to grips with the realization of how sick he had been. All day he stewed about the future and whether or not "I'm going to get out of here."

My parents arrived in the early afternoon and, for the first time, were allowed to see Jack. Judging by their facial expressions, they were stunned. While I had seen changes each day, they suddenly were witnessing his weight loss, the dark circles, and jaundiced skin.

Jack's emotions were also in a dire state. He was cranky, cynical, and not very friendly. As if he were hiding from the devil in the far corner of a prison cell, he mentally withdrew from the conversation. Obviously, he was not ready for visitors. Later, I asked him if he wanted to call the boys and Barbara. He replied, "I'm not ready yet, maybe in a few days."

The brief unsettling visit with Jack didn't help my mother's mood. She had entered the hospital feeling angry. My dad had parked the car at a meter to save the extra fifty cents he would have spent in the parking garage.

When my parents left the hospital, their car was buried in a mountain of fresh snow. The Ford Galaxie would not budge and the motor died in the process. My normally calm mother stormed back into the hospital to tell me their plight while Daddy called AAA. When the snow was finally shoveled away and the car excavated from its burial ground, their usual fifteen minute drive home took almost four hours.

By the time my parents arrived at their apartment, I was on my way to dinner with old friends, Jane and John Billington.

They picked me up at six o'clock and we drove to an old St. Louis establishment, Stan & Biggies, named after Stan Musial of St. Louis Cardinal Baseball fame.

As we entered the restaurant, I spotted a telephone booth and excused myself to call my parents. My mother was still angry, but glad to be safely home. I could now enjoy my second night on the town.

The sharing of good food and conversation with Jack's longtime friends was refreshing. They had become my friends as well. A tall, wiry grey-haired man, John was a highly respected real estate developer, and an international traveler. His wife, Jane, was a jovial spirit, dedicated volunteer, and community leader. A tall woman, at least five-foot-ten, she had short, closely cropped blond hair, most likely dyed, and wore dark, horn-rimmed glasses. Jane was also a reformed alcoholic.

She enjoyed a cup of coffee before dinner while John and I sipped on a dry gin martini, my favorite drink, and my first in over two weeks. It tasted like ice-cold liquid velvet as it swirled around my mouth and down my throat. When John asked if I wanted a second, I accepted. Goodness, I thought, it could be weeks before I would have another. We all enjoyed the Stan and Biggies specialty–T-bone steak followed by New York cheese cake. It was the most nutritious and delicious meal I had enjoyed in months, and I hoped it would give me renewed strength.

The relaxing, give-and-take conversation revolved around Jack's health, our children, and our life at Muskingum, Jane's fight with alcoholism, and John's plans for hunting in Siberia. After a warm and wonderful evening, the knots in my stomach disappeared.

It was after ten o'clock by the time I returned to the hospital. Jack had just watched "Columbo." A big smile appeared on his face when I entered the room. Thank god he didn't ask "Where the hell have you been?" That retort would have made me feel guilty. After a brief chat about dinner with Jane and John, a big bear hug, and an emotionally charged kiss, we reluctantly said goodnight. I would be in the next room, but it seemed like hundreds of miles from his arms.

I yearned to climb in his bed. With our starving bodies to keep each other warm, we could close out the world and take a long winter's nap. The nurses might have been surprised, but it would have been fun. We were sorely in need of a good laugh.

As it turned out, with several new and very sick patients in the ICU, the night was unusually noisy, and neither one of us had a good sleep. The bright lights were as hot as the noon day sun. Perspiration flowed, as doctors and nurses scurried here and there, desperately striving to save lives.

I retrieved my pillow and blanket from my locker and escaped to my empty waiting room. I settled in to read a medical journal that I had borrowed from one of the doctors. I was desperate to know all the specifics of cardiomyopathy, because I might be Jack's primary care giver if he ever left the hospital. I remember thinking, as I drifted off to sleep, "I must ask one of the interns to teach me how to read the EKG tapes."

As if I had been struck by lightening, I awoke with a start. Another code blue was announced over the intercom. Never will I forget the thunderous sound of the crash cart rolling on the highly polished terrazzo floors, and the running feet, getting louder and louder as they neared cardiac intensive care. Nurses and doctors from all corners of the hospital threw open the double doors leading into the ICU. I trembled in utter fear.

Fortunately, it was another patient, but the night was still a long and frightening one for Jack. His increasing nightmares were so terrifying that he couldn't talk about them. Sylvia said this was not unusual when a person is confined to four walls for an extended period of time. She referred to Jack's bad dreams as "environmental nightmares," which are caused by many things— the glare of bright lights, beeps from heart monitors, hissing respirators, and constant interruptions to take blood pressure, temperature, pulse, etc. In spite of the nightmares, Jack told one of the doctors, "I think I'm making progress."

Day 16

Day sixteen brought a new assessment. A gravity test, patented by Dr. Rainey, measured the contraction and flow of blood to and from the heart. Jack passed with flying colors. Another first: he ate his meals sitting on his "doughnut hole."

Jack was terribly embarrassed, but he was suffering from old-fashioned bed sores. The nurses had tried everything from an air mattress to a soft sheepskin rug, but only the "doughnut hole" eased the pain.

Day 17

On the last day of January, Jack awoke starving; the breakfast tray couldn't arrive soon enough. While each day continued one step at a time, he appeared to have more energy. Every day, he coughed up sputum and, when he couldn't get it all out, it scared him. He thought he was choking. Rainey assured him that his lungs would clear soon.

Much to my pleasant surprise, Dr. Rainey said that we would soon begin planning Jack's re-entry into the real world. "It will be regimented," he said. I wondered what that meant. It sounded like strict discipline with no flexibility.

As Jack's body continued to stabilize and gain strength, the crises subsided, and the daily rhythm became more relaxed. There were exercises with the physical therapist, and meals served promptly every four hours.

Jack's secretary had sent our personal mail each week, so now that Jack was feeling better, it was time for me to catch up with note writing and paying bills. Writing checks in the best of times is a chore, but in the hospital it was even more difficult.

We had also received a draft report on the St. Lawrence University trip. It required proof reading and editing before returning in the next day's mail. I read the report aloud to Jack. He made a few minor changes, and I edited for grammar and punctuation. This was the first time that Jack was able to cope with anything work-related.

The future was seldom discussed. Most evenings were spent holding hands or rubbing his back, quietly watching television, reading get-well cards, or talking with friends on the telephone. The volumes of get-well cards that arrived each day brought tears to Jack's eyes and mine, too.

Out of nowhere, people we had not seen or heard from in several years, and who had just learned of Jack's illness, called. There was the mother of a professor, former college roommates and other old friends, and the wonderful black man who had been Jack's butler at Lindenwood. Where they got the phone number for "my little phone booth," I did not know. Although I loved each and every call, I began to find long conversations physically and mentally exhausting. I seemed to be saying the same thing over and over again. As Jack's vitality improved, I spent less time on the phone and more time with him.

I recall one evening when we watched the birth of "Black

Beauty." Jack and I were horse lovers, so we were thrilled to view a childhood favorite together. It prompted a telephone call to Steve, our country neighbor. We were anxious to know if Echo's pregnancy was proceeding smoothly. Steve said she was fine and that "her sides are beginning to swell." A native born Ohio farmer, Steve cut and baled our hay field in the summer, at no cost to us. We had more than enough for our mare, as well as to supplement hay for his cattle during the winter months. It was a good arrangement from which we all benefited.

After hanging up the phone, Jack and I found ourselves unexpectedly in a nostalgic mood. "Jack loves the farm so much," I wrote in my journal that night. We were anxious for spring, so we could go home to the farm. Our cottage had been completed in the fall, but there were still numerous finishing touches to be done.

Day 18

The first day of February awoke following a rough night of nightmares for Jack. He shared his visions of Empress Katherine playing Russian liturgical music on an organ. I wondered who Katherine was and thought that maybe he was dreaming about a previous incarnation. Whatever, he was not able to shake the memory, and his bad dreams galloped into a frightening morning.

Excessive lung congestion returned, along with shortness of breath and elevated blood pressure. His heart rate was 130 with atrial flutter. I did not know the meaning of atrial flutter, but it was frightening to observe. Fortunately, the injection of a diuretic and a carotid sinus massage slowed everything down. Jack was exhausted and slept all afternoon.

A pleasant surprise occurred when Father Paul Reinert, president of Saint Louis University, came to visit. Alas, Jack was sleeping and I didn't want to wake him. As Father Reinert gave me a peck on the cheek, he whispered that he would return another day.

Paul Reinert and Jack had become close friends and comrades during Jack's presidency of the Missouri Association of Private Colleges and Universities. Together they'd initiated and implemented a scholarship program that enabled Missouri students to attend any private college or university in the state–the first of its kind in the country. Jack was disappointed, to say the least, when he awoke to find that he had slept through Father Reinert's visit.

He continued to be confused and disoriented, so after dinner that evening I went to the hospital drugstore and purchased a new Timex watch. Chuckling, he said, "It will help me to know when you have overslept." My main goal had been to help him differentiate the time of day or night, thus lessening the possibility of nightmares. He had become so afraid to sleep that he wanted to watch television into the wee hours.

After watching the second installment of "Black Beauty," he said, "If you'll stay with me all night, I'll give you the foal." How I wanted to crawl in beside him and feel the warmth of his body. What ecstasy that would have been. And sex—what was that? It had been so long. Love-making in cardiac intensive would have been ludicrous, but it also would have been bliss. I kissed Jack goodnight, wrote in my journal for awhile, then turned out the light, hoping to sleep, but that was not to be.

A code blue was announced over the speaker system and the crash cart came barreling down the hall, like a fire truck with its lights flashing. The overhead light came on and the family of the new patient entered 'my room.' Dr. Ganga politely asked me to leave, so that he could talk with the family. I paced the empty corridors, and checked on the sleeping Jack until the doctor left. It was after midnight and I could barely keep my eyes open. Although the family of the new patient was still there–four or five in number–I curled up on my sofa with the blanket over my head and was off to dreamland. Across the room, the distant voices sounded like chattering chipmunks.

My dreams that night were unusually vivid, as if they were really happening. Jack and I, locked in each others arms, were at our cabin deep in the Maine woods. Although the cabin on Lake Echo had long since been sold, neither of us would ever forget the two idyllic months spent there in the summer of 1973. God had blessed us. We boated, cooked and ate fresh lobster and scallops all summer. On rainy days, we made love in the morning and went antiquing and barn sale shopping in the afternoon. Who could ever have dreamt of a more heavenly honeymoon? Never again would we share such precious moments, completely alone.

Day 19

After a night of beautiful dreams, I awoke to find that Jack had had his best sleep yet, no nightmares. For the first time in seventeen days, he realized where he was, and slowly began to ask questions about what had transpired during the previous weeks. When Dr. Naki, the kidney specialist, stopped by, Jack heard for the first time about the peritoneal dialysis treatment. His facial expression was one of complete disbelief. His mouth fell open and his eyes looked at me in dismay, like a frightened owl in the night. "That could not have happened to me," he said. "Oh, but it did," I replied, "for seventeen long hours by the tick, tick, tick of the clock with gallons of water gushing in and out of your body." He was shocked at the mere thought.

We talked for hours about the thin grey line he had traveled between life and death since January 15. He wanted every detail. The dialysis treatment had saved his life; his kidneys were back to normal function.

Later that day, Jack had a multitude of questions for Dr. Rainey. "What about my weight? What about my heart rate? When can I get out of here? Am I going to be able to return to my work?" This was his first rational conversation with the doctor, and the words flowed—stream of consciousness questions with no end.

Jack was horrified at his drop in weight from 180 lbs. to 161 lbs., but Rainey wanted him to maintain that level. His heart rate was still in atrial flutter. Rainey hoped he could continue to tolerate the pace. The fluctuating situation was a vicious circle. If Rainey tried to convert the rate to normal sinus rhythm it would, no doubt, revert to fibrillation eventually. That had been the pattern. Now that his kidneys were back to normal, the jaundiced eyes had disappeared.

The doctor said, "Now all he needs is lots of sleep and rest. He'll probably be in the ICU another three to five days." Before leaving, Rainey added a new item to Jack's diet: ice cream. Jack's eyes lit up like a kid in the candy store.

All in all, it was a good news day. The doctor had given Jack reason to have a positive outlook for the future. He would have another good night of sleep as well, but I would not.

Day 20

Just before dawn, I awakened with a start to hear loud voices nearby. Evidently, a new patient and his or her family had arrived during the night. The family was emotionally upset and frustrated as they waited to see the doctor. The wife said, "He'll be out in three hours." I did not know whether she meant the doctor or her husband, but I presumed the latter.

Chuckling to myself, I pulled the covers over my head. In 1978, the usual hospital stay for an uncomplicated heart attack was one week in intensive care, followed by two weeks in a regular room. Twenty-five years later, cardiac patients are sent home within a few days.

How I wished Jack and I could go home. On the other hand, home is not a place or a house or a city, but rather home is where your heart is, and my heart was with Jack. He was my home, my lover, and my security blanket. We were blessed. Our love, our work, and our lives were all entwined like some giant jigsaw puzzle. Our life at Muskingum College was like a dream coming true. Every day I prayed we would soon return to our family, our friends, and the place we had come to love.

We had just received good news from the college. Rupert, the academic dean, called to say that the faculty retreat at Salt Fork State Park was going well. The mood of the faculty was upbeat and positive. A very proper person and a former minister, Rupert held his trim figure erect whether in casual conversation or conducting a faculty meeting. His warm, friendly eyes and calm demeanor were a good fit for his role as dean, and a compatible contrast for Jack. Through Rupert's stable and supportive leadership, the college had moved ahead in Jack's absence.

Thinking back, it was remarkable that, during their conversation, Jack was able to convey a message to the faculty. He dictated the following communication, "God bless you all. I'll be back. My doctor is being cautious." The dean also shared a get-well message from John Harrison, a member of the board, requesting that I call him.

When John answered the phone, his booming voice yelled, "How's my buddy?" If only he knew, I thought. A steel company executive, John was one of Jack's favorite people. With warm eyes and stocky build, John was a gregarious and generous human being who loved Jack Brown. The feeling was mutual. While John was a golfer and Jack was not, they shared the same first name, a love of politics, laughter, and a good dry martini. John liked his Russian vodka ice cold and on the rocks with only a splash of water; Jack preferred Bombay Gin. They had to share their vice privately, for alcohol, at that time, was not allowed in public places on Muskingum's campus. After a delightful conversation, it was time for Jack to rest; he was exhausted.

Later that afternoon, before I left to celebrate my father's seventy-second birthday, Jack asked me to get Bill on the phone. He wanted to find out how things were going. Jack was so proud of Bill and the way he had handled the crisis. In the course of their chat, Bill expressed concern about making applications for college. Although he could have gone to Muskingum tuition-free, he wanted a larger university with a more diverse student body. His preferences were Bowling Green State University and Miami University of Ohio. I promised we would make appointments and visit those institutions as soon as I could get home.

Time was of the essence, particularly at Miami, which closed admissions in early spring. Since the president of Miami and his wife were friends, I told Bill I would call to make arrangements. That confirmation seemed to alleviate his concerns, at least for the time being. I prayed Jack would be well enough to join us on those trips, but that was not meant to be.

Eventually, Bill and I visited Bowling Green and Miami Universities. The latter was Bill's choice, but by the time we visited, the class was filled for the fall term. He enrolled the following January, and graduated four years later with a degree in physical education. While he was not able to play basketball, he had a rewarding experience on the lacrosse team, making life-long friends. Jack would have been proud of his stepson.

Day 21

February Fourth dawned and was Jack's third consecutive day with no shortness of breath. Hallelujah. Like he was on a merry-go-round and didn't know where to get off, Jack was suddenly talking non-stop. He asked questions of the nurses, and quizzed me incessantly. His brain was operating at full capacity and he was beginning to worry about everything.

First, it was talk about Lindenwood, its faculty, and his unwanted departure from that institution. Then, it was fast forward to Muskingum with all of its attributes and concerns. How in the world, I thought, am I going to calm him down? The continual chatter was out of control.

It didn't help matters when the mail arrived in my absence, and Jack learned of the unexpected death of one of his faculty members. The Dean had shared the news with me earlier, but I'd thought it best not to tell Jack. The tragedy did not disturb him outwardly, but deep in his psyche I knew he was thinking about his own mortality.

When Jack received this news, I was enjoying a spirited luncheon with colleagues recently retired from Lindenwood. Mary Lichliter and Lula Clayton Beale, devoted friends, had been ecstatic when Jack and I married. I had known both women when I was a student. Mary was the dean of students for over thirty years, and Lula Clayton, the college registrar, almost as long.

Had it not been for Mary, I might never have worked at the college and, hence, might never have known Jack. Upon Mary's recommendation, I had been hired by the previous president to be the alumnae director. Mary took me under her wing. Then, I followed in her footsteps as acting dean of students after she retired.

Mary and Lula Clayton often invited Jack and me for cocktails. After our marriage, we reciprocated over dinner with Jack's special Bombay Gin martinis, served very cold and very dry, followed by beef brisket–my mother's recipe–and hours of stimulating conversation. Mary, originally from New England, and Lula Clayton, from Kentucky, warmed our hearts and fed our souls. We loved them dearly.

On that day, it was wonderful to see two such special friends–both in their seventies, but chipper as ever. Mary had wavy, coiffed brown hair speckled with gray, and wore wire-rimmed glasses over her intense blue-gray eyes. Her stature had always been commanding, but as she aged her demeanor had mellowed.

Lula Clayton was a gentle soul who loved to laugh. In spite of a childhood illness which had left one side of her face partially paralyzed, her eyes twinkled and there was not a mean thought circulating through her brain. At five-foot-ten with a trim figure, she wore beautiful silk dresses which accentuated her short, spiffy hair style.

We ate little lunch, but the conversation was non-stop. I had not seen the two women since Jack and I had moved to Ohio, so we had lots of catching up to do. But, of course, the prime focus of our conversation revolved around Jack. Mary and Lula Clayton loved Jack like a mother loves a son. Not being able to think about anything but Jack, like a homing pigeon, I was anxious to return to the hospital.

Jack demanded a complete replay of the luncheon conversation. And then, he was off and running about this subject and that, worrying about the past, the future, and things he could do nothing about. Shortly thereafter, his blood pressure sky-rocketed, and by nightfall, he had a pounding headache.

Dr. Rainey stopped in for a chat on his way home. Jack was already asleep for the night. Rainey shared with me his recommendation that we stay in St. Louis for at least a week after Jack's dismissal from the hospital. He also suggested that we go to a warmer climate for several months, perhaps Arizona, before returning to Ohio.

My heart soared with excitement. Where would we stay in St. Louis, I thought? There was my parents' apartment, and we had many friends, but I was concerned for Jack's need for absolute rest. The best option was a hotel where a special cardiac diet could be ordered, and access to other services would be available including an elevator.

The big question was, who did we know in Arizona or New Mexico? Jack's son, Philip, had lived in Albuquerque for several years, but he and his family had recently moved to California. The only person we knew in Arizona was Jack's long time friend and colleague, Emil MacGuire who served on the Muskingum Board of Trustees. Emil and his wife lived in Tucson and I was confident that they would be delighted to suggest an apartment complex where we could rent a one bedroom unit for several months.

Although I was excited at the prospect of a trip to Arizona, my rational mind told me it was only a dream. When Jack got stronger, we would discuss crossing the bridge to the outside world. I made a mental note to chat about Arizona with Jack and then, perhaps, we would call Emil. After the long cold winter, we were both starved for sunshine and warm weather, and Jack sorely needed the nourishment of the great outdoors. I was eager, but knew that restraint had to be my guide.

That evening, I read and wrote in my journal late into the night.

Day 22

I was startled when Anna, one of the nurses, woke me from a deep sleep. My immediate reaction was one of alarm. I feared something had happened to Jack. "Heavens," Anna said, "Jack sent me to wake you up. He thinks it is time for you to arise."

As if the sunlight had scrolled through his body, igniting his mind, he was cheerful, happy, and anxious to see me. I was ecstatic to find him in such joy, and responded with a long, sexy kiss and a bear hug. He had already had breakfast and was awaiting the arrival of his physical therapist. I knew he would be in good hands, so I blew him a kiss and was off to make myself presentable. When I hugged him, I felt the thin layer of skin covering his ribs, as transparent as parchment paper, any fat or muscle tissue was nonexistent. I thought, "I'm going to feed Jack more than he's getting in this hospital."

While changing my clothes in the nurses' locker room, I observed that I, also, had shed a few pounds. My clothes were hanging loose, my cheeks were hollow, and the pallor of my skin lacked its usual color and resilience. Oh, well, not to worry–make-up would hide the flaws.

Of greater concern was my wardrobe. There is a limit to what you can mix and match with only five outfits of clothing. The sweaters, including several turtlenecks, were different colors: my favorites, red and black, and there was also white, cranberry, and gray. I wore a different sweater each day for five days and then rotated. There was also a choice of skirt or slacks. Although what I wore was unimportant, for the first time in several weeks, I was thinking about clothing.

What if I persuaded my mother to take me shopping? I had become aware that I was subconsciously looking for opportunities to leave the hospital. I was definitely suffering from cabin fever. After dressing quickly and applying a touch of make-up and lipstick, I hurried off to meet Jeanette and two of her friends, who were also respiratory therapists.

They had become very fond of Jack, and invited me to join them for breakfast in the coffee shop. Their primary job as respiratory therapists was to assist patients with the draining of their pulmonary cavity. I called them "the pounders." Using the fist and the side of their hand, they spent ten or fifteen minutes each visit pounding on Jack's chest, loosening any phlegm.

The pounders were bubbling, charming, and very good at

their profession. I don't remember what we talked about that morning, but I have fond memories of the warmth and friendship they extended to me during a very difficult time. I was filled with gratitude for so many caring friends. The therapists hurried off to work, and I made my way to the hospital chapel for some quiet time.

The Episcopal chapel radiated light with a striking stained-glass window depicting the life of Jesus. Only the altar and the brilliant window were lit by the rays from a soft overhead light. There were five rows of red velvet cushioned pews. I often stopped at the chapel and came to relish the solitude and contentment in the quiet space.

Early in my hospital stay, not knowing whether Jack was going to live or die, I was numb to the rest of the world. Like the tide on the beach flowing in and out, I simply rolled from one crisis to the next. My heart was not open. I prayed, but I was never sure if God heard me. On that morning, I knew. Jack was alive and gaining strength with each day.

As I knelt in prayer, my heart overflowed with gratitude and joy for Jack's love. Although I had grown up in a loving family, I must confess that, before Jack came into my life, I had never experienced the depth of emotion, the out-pouring of affection, and the passion we came to share as our relationship grew. It transcended the self and went far beyond anything I had ever known. We were so intuitive and sensitive to each other that it was scary to realize another human being could read my mind.

For me, Jack represented a powerful ideal of what true love can be, if we only reach out to others. I would carry this ideal with me forever and do my utmost to pass the torch of love, the caring, and compassion on to family and friends. Jack made me feel as Elizabeth Barrett Browning must have felt when she wrote, "He loved her into full being."

***

In my early years, I never imagined that I would one day give a speech on the meaning of love. It happened during our second year at Muskingum, when I was invited to speak at the weekly vesper service. My meditation was entitled "The Greatest of These Is Love." The basis of my remarks was Henry Drummond's analysis of Paul's description of love, as found in First Corinthians, verse 13. I raised the question to the assembled students, faculty, and administrators:

> "Are students here learning how to love? Not how to receive love, but how to give it. You can have all the knowledge there is, but if you don't have love in your heart, you have nothing. You can't be a good doctor, teacher, poet, artist, or lawyer if you don't know how to love. We all know those who have it—they are radiant, they are transformed, and they take time to be kind. We also know those who don't have it—the lonely people who build walls instead of bridges. They may commit suicide, they may steal things, and they sometimes commit crimes of violence. They need you and me to love them."

After Jack's death, a letter from a friend eloquently expressed my feelings, "Great love will always ask a great price from us, but it is such a glorious blessing."

I meditated longer than I realized, more than an hour, so I sprinted from the chapel, taking the stairs two at a time to the second floor. Jack wondered where I had been, but I was pleased that he had a visitor. His favorite doctor, Maria, had walked from her hospital room, the first trip without her wheel chair. She was amazed at Jack's improvement and thought he looked better than on his previous hospital visit.

She, too, had significantly improved and anticipated going home within a few days. How we would miss her. I had enjoyed Maria's company and luxuriated in the warmth of her shower. I wondered what I would do. Perhaps, Jack would soon be moved to his own private room with a bath. My intuition told me it would happen, if not today, in the near future.

While awaiting word from Dr. Rainey as to whether or not the move would occur, an exceptionally ill patient arrived in the adjacent cubicle. What a miraculous and amazing story his wife shared with me. Her husband suffered from a severely irritated fibrotic heart muscle and had endured open heart surgery at the University of Chicago. The surgeons had used a special needle to explore his heart muscle, inch by inch, cutting out the irritated tissue along the way. Every time they cut away a piece of the diseased muscle, his heart went into ventricular tachycardia. His wife lived in the waiting room for six months.

What was I complaining about, I pondered? I had only been hibernating for three weeks.

As the day wore on, Jack became increasingly fretful and depressed. His nerves were obviously at the surface and ready to explode. I was afraid to bring up any subject for fear he would take off on some tangent. Frivolous topics were out of the question while he was stewing about this and that: what was happening at the college in his absence, the college's finances, as well as our own, the farm, the new house, the children, et cetera.

He knew that on the following day the executive committee of the board of trustees would be meeting. If only he'd understood how much love those men and women had for him, he might not have been such a worrywart.

At a most appropriate moment, Carol, one of the therapists, came for his daily workout. While she pounded, I read some devotional passages to Jack. The combination of therapies seemed to relax his mind and elevate his spirits.

Soon after, he admitted the reason for his depression. Dr. Rainey had indicated he might be moved out of the ICU, but it had not happened. The doctor told me later that he did not want to jar the "good luck." I also believed he did not want Jack to have regular access to the telephone.

When Maria had been there earlier, she indicated the staff had superstitions about Jack's room, #2608. The room is always set aside for the extremely ill; every patient has always recovered. With such positive experience, why couldn't he just stay in the same room, I wondered? Later in the day, for the first time, the doctor allowed Jack to take a few steps. This lifted his spirit and confidence level, temporarily.

Day 23

Alas, the next morning dawned and he was still on the worry track. He tormented himself about whether or not he would be able to return to Muskingum. For him, it was "Me college." All day, his heart rate went up and down with shortness of breath and terrible chest pain. Then, suddenly, everything would go back to normal and the pain would subside. He walked a fine line, teetering between life and death. I was frightened and did not leave his bedside the entire day.

Somehow, I wanted to discover a way to lessen the stress. The doctor said he should never again take Valium or any kind of sedative that would lower the blood pressure. Although Rainey said it was premature to predict what Jack was going to be able to do, he also said the college needed his mind, not his body. His goal was to release Jack from the hospital within two weeks. Wow, that was good news. The doctor was obviously pleased with Jack's progress and somewhat optimistic, which gave me hope.

For the first time in over three weeks, Jack sat in a chair to eat his dinner of unseasoned roasted chicken breast, parsley potatoes, and mixed vegetables. We watched Dean Martin's roast of Frank Sinatra. Jack laughed, real gut-wrenching belly laughs, for over an hour. It was good to see him happy, but, by nine o'clock, his heart rate soared to 130 in atrial flutter with supraventricular tachycardia. It was midnight by the time his heart rhythm returned to normal and sleep descended. I was so worried that I remained at his bedside, reading and writing in my journal long into the night.

Day 24

When I awoke early the next morning, I wondered if I would be able to shower. The previous day, I had hoped to have a bath and change of clothes, but it never happened. Jack had not had a good day and did not want to be alone, so the shower had to wait. And so, there I was rolling out of bed in the same clothes I had put on forty-eight hours before. I felt awful and looked even worse. I quickly folded up my blanket, brushed my hair, and hurried to see Jack. He was nervous and fidgety, and I knew immediately the heart rate might surge again. And, so might mine.

A short time later, I had a quick breakfast in the coffee shop. As I listened to the continual stream of messages over the paging system, I was ridden with anxiety. I was sure my normally low blood pressure was sky high. Filled with apprehension, I returned to find Jack's heart rate off the charts. Finally, after a roller coaster morning, things returned to normal around one o'clock.

Although it was mid afternoon, I left to have a bath and head wash, and my last chat with Maria. She was glad to be going home. I would never forget her many kindnesses, and always would treasure her memory. But, frankly, at that moment, I wondered where I would shower next.

Chapter VI

TURNING OUT THE LIGHT

"The girl with the beautiful black hair, I'll never forget you."
–*John Anthony Brown*

Day 25

The next morning, Jack, now rational and alert, sent one of the nurses to awaken me. "She has slept long enough," I was told. While Jack had been making up for lost time in the sleep department, my nights were interrupted by distraught families coming and going from the waiting room. Anguished spouses and children wanted to talk when I was writing or trying to sleep; visiting bed fellows snored like owls hooting in the night, or the code blue crash cart barreled down the corridor, hell bent for a dying patient's bedside. I often wished for the smell of fragrant flowers to bring hope and warmth to the dismal atmosphere.

Was I lonely? Not really. While I longed for the heat of Jack's body, he was in the next room. When he was asleep and the waiting room was crowded with suffering families, I lived in my own world, with my own thoughts, and my writing. As if I were crossing a bridge over the Mississippi, my words were the wheels carrying me across the fright of the deep waters beneath. What I didn't know then, I understand now. My writings may have distanced me from reality, but they also enabled me to face the unfolding drama before me.

As Jack improved, he either slept for hours, or he fretted about when he was going to move out of the ICU. As if he were a baby, each day he moved forward two steps and back one. As long as there was evidence of improvement, I had hope. Not having any idea his days were numbered, the doctors kept inching his treatment toward recovery.

Day 26

The big day finally arrived. Jack was moved via wheelchair to Room 2502, a regular room with an outside window, a shower, and a roll-a-way bed. After twenty-five days of depressing hospital green, the new room was refreshing in daffodil yellow with tan, green, and gold plaid curtains draping the picture window. Jack was so excited his heart rate rocketed briefly. Breathing on his own again, he spent the next seven hours without needing additional oxygen.

Although we had said goodbye to our favorite ICU nurses, we were pleased with the head nurse in 2500–she was a doll. Nurse Diane was a tall, statuesque brunette who always dressed in a freshly pressed white uniform, navy blue sweater, white hose, and freshly polished white shoes. Her long hair was piled on her head and held in place with a heavily starched nurse's cap signifying she was a graduate of Kent State University's nursing program. She had a snappy stride and always a smile. She radiated happiness to her patients.

On special holidays, Diane dressed for the occasion, bringing laughter to her patients, their families, and visitors, as well. In celebration of Valentine's Day, she wore a pink uniform, a red cupid's arrow decorated her cap, and her stethoscope was heart-shaped. She told me that on Halloween, she wears black with a Groucho Marx mask. She was an expert at inserting IV's and Jack never felt the needle.

Days 27-28

In addition to Diane's loving care, the next few days were filled with love and joy from family and a multitude of friends. Phone conversations with Jack's three sons, daughter, and stepson took place. Son Philip was on a business trip from California and made a surprise visit. My parents were able to see Jack each day, and I enjoyed a long anticipated luncheon at Jeremiah's Restaurant in Kirkwood with my mother and her life-long friend, Irene Bleckschmidt.

A charming, vivacious woman of German heritage, Irene lived more than ninety years. She never failed to remember my birthday. Not having children of her own, she treated me as if I were her daughter. She was extremely concerned about Jack, because her husband, Bleck, had died of the same heart condition, in the same hospital. Needless to say, our conversation on that day revolved around Jack and Bleck. Following Jeremiah's special chicken salad with grapes and walnuts, and homemade cloverleaf rolls, Mother and I said goodbye to Irene, then headed for Frontenac Plaza, an upscale suburban shopping mall in St. Louis County.

Valentine's Day was approaching and I wanted something

special to wear for Jack. After much deliberation, I selected a red silk blouse with a white plaid overlay and a contrasting scarf. It felt soft and sexy against my skin. I was excited to wear something new, so I asked the sales clerk to put my old gray sweater in a sack and I wore my new blouse back to the hospital. Jack loved it.

Day 29

Sharing his love for words, my Valentine gift to him was the newly released *The Thornbirds,* a saga about an Australian family, by Colleen McCullough. For the next two evenings, Jack and I shared enjoyable stories of the outback. He sometimes fell asleep while I was reading. I would never forget those last special hours together. *The Thornbirds,* with its beautiful and courageous love story, would become a new friend in the days, months, and years ahead. It was almost as if I continued to share the story with Jack, in hopes he was listening. I'm confident his spirit was right there with me.

Day 30

What was to be my husband's last day in this life began on a positive note. Jack awoke refreshed, had a sponge bath, and a nice breakfast. However, as the hours wore on, he became restless and frightened. At first, I was confused. Did he know something I didn't?

Then, it became evident. A short walk around the room sent his heart rate escalating, and eating lunch caused pain in his stomach, and rhythm fluctuations. He couldn't even digest his food.

Obviously, he had overdone the walking, so it was back to a prone position. He sat on the side of the single bed in his Roman velour robe. As if it were yesterday, I still can see the disappointment in his eyes and the thin, gray pallor of his cheeks. My heart sank to a bottomless pit. He had come so far. I told him we were not going to give up now. He had so hoped to walk down the hospital corridor, but that was not what God had planned.

One of his favorite physicians, Michael Trenor, made a surprise visit in the late afternoon. Michael had been on duty during our first two weeks at St. Luke's. Evidently, he had called and learned Jack had been upgraded to another room. I remember what a joy it was for Jack to see Michael again. Tall and blue-eyed with sandy hair, Mark and his wife had a new baby girl.

He proudly showed us the latest pictures, and also surprised me with a gift–a gin martini. How Jack would have loved one, but he couldn't eat his dinner, much less have a drink.

We shared a few laughs as I sipped the martini. How good it was to see Jack with a smile on his face. After Michael's departure, Jack kissed me and quietly murmured, "The girl with the beautiful black hair, I'll never forget you." Later, I wondered if he made a conscious choice to die at that moment. While I was still fighting for his life, he clearly knew his body did not have the strength to go on.

Dinner arrived and, after a few bites of mashed potatoes and strawberry Jell-O, he pushed the tray away and lay back on the bed, exhausted. He didn't have the energy and he also was afraid to eat. I, too, was in need of nourishment, but didn't want to leave Jack alone. So I proceeded to eat his baked chicken, lumpy mashed potatoes, and green peas. With his head reclined, Jack watched my every mouthful while my stomach did flip-flops. I was so frightened it's a wonder I didn't choke on my food.

When I finished eating, Jack asked me to read a few pages from *The Thornbirds*. Then, he became extremely weary and drifted off to sleep.

A nurse I had never seen before came to check his vitals. His temperature was hovering around 101, the pulse was fast and barely audible, and the blood pressure was very low. By that time, I was so fearful that I actually trembled deep inside. Not knowing what to think or what to do, I took a short walk down the corridor. Visiting hours were over, lights were dim, and it was ghostly silent except for the whispered voices of nurses and orderlies.

When I returned to the room a few minutes later, Jack was suddenly gripped with an electric charge defying anything I had ever witnessed. He thrashed aimlessly about, and heaving gasps bellowed from his lungs. Nurses came running as Jack went into convulsions, instantly followed by cardiac arrest. By the time the crash cart arrived, the essence of Jack Brown's persona was gone forever. But his beautiful mind was not willing to give up—the brain waves continued on.

As my heart plummeted to the depths of despair, Jack lasted through the night and into the early morning hours. Until his reflexes shut down and his brain cells ceased to function, I sat by his bed, massaging his cold hands, and wiping his brow. Sobbing most of the night, I quietly talked about the extraordinary life we had shared, albeit brief.

For twelve years, our relationship had been central to our work, and for six years, the center of every thought–indeed the essence of our existence. What was I going to do, where was I to go without him? As if my emotions had flowed out to sea with the tide, by morning my nerves were hopelessly shredded, raw, and completely drained.

Slowly, the brain wave monitor gave way to a straight line. Jack's cheeks were cold to the touch, and his lips were silent, never again to utter a word. His bright light had been turned off, but his spirit would remain deep within my soul. He had eclipsed his body to live in the great universe of stars.

My recollection of our last conversation hovers in the distance, like a thought barely remembered—out of reach as in a dream. I try to grasp it, but it eludes me.

At that moment, I felt detached from my own body and I don't recall if I contacted my parents, or someone else did, but suddenly they appeared. Jack's light had just gone out, and I was no doubt visibly exhausted. As if I were a single oyster washed up on the beach, never had I felt so lost and alone. I kissed Jack's cold unresponsive lips goodbye, then hugged my waiting parents. Blinded by tears and functioning only God knows how, I retrieved my clothes and packed the suitcase.

Nurse Diane appeared with Jack's meager belongings in a plain brown paper bag. She wore her long flowing hair in a chignon, and carried her lithe body with grace. I had asked Diane to leave Jack's wedding band in place, but to give me his silver-initialed ring and his gold watch. I planned to give the ring to Anthony, the eldest son.

After giving Diane a hug and thanking her for the caring way in which she took care of Jack, suddenly, out of the blue, my nerves splintered and rose to the surface. It was as if my body had disconnected and the fabric of my tummy had erupted in a gnawing uneasiness. As I prepared to leave the safe haven of the hospital–my home for thirty days–I was afraid. Diane asked if I would like a Valium. I declined.

I hurriedly said goodbye to what seemed like an endless sea of medical staff. They had been so kind, supportive, and loving. Jack had been more than a patient to them; he was their friend and they cared what happened to him. I would not soon forget their tears.

It was time to leave, but I didn't want to go. My parents waited patiently by the elevator. By the time we reached the first floor, my nervous system was in severe turmoil. My heart was racing and my knees were shaking.

Abruptly, I turned to my parents and told them I had forgotten to tell my friends in the ICU goodbye. I hit the up button for the elevator, exited on the second floor, and headed for the nurses' station. There was Diane, in conversation with one of the resident physicians. I said "I think I need a Valium after all." Although she knew I had the remainder of Jack's Valium in my suitcase, she gave me four tablets to get me home.

While I desperately was in need of something to calm my nerves, I secretly hoped Dr. Rainey might have arrived on the floor. It was a big disappointment that my two favorite people, Dr. Rainey and Nurse Sylvia, were not on duty at the time of my departure.

Sylvia was on a much needed vacation, reclining on a sunny beach in Puerto Rico. She told me once that the stress level in the cardiac ICU was so great that, every six weeks, she took ten days to go to the beach for rest and relaxation. Although Sylvia was not there the day Jack died, she wrote to me later:

> "I remember walking into work last Saturday night and thinking what a good evening it was going to be. There were no critically ill or unstable patients in the unit. Well, we soon got one new patient, quickly followed by another. The second patient coded at 11:30. We all worked frantically to save him, but without success. I went home at 3:00 a.m., missing a friend's party, very depressed, and wondering why we hadn't the power to save this patient.
>
> I came into work the next day, still a little down, but glad to be there. We received a new patient around 10:45 p.m. She coded at 11:40 and died. I felt especially sad, because five minutes before her arrest, she had asked me to have them stop all the sticking and poking; to just let her die peaceably. I reassured her that she wasn't going to die. How wrong I was. What gave me the almighty right to say when her death was or wasn't going to occur. I went home that night even more exhausted than the night before.
>
> The next morning I went to class and, while ignoring my history lecturer, I pondered the thought of possibly being in the wrong profession. The medical field was definitely wearing on me. It

isn't like the business world where, if you fail, a little money is lost or, politics, where if you fail, you lose your job.

Medicine has the privilege of being the only profession where if you fail, someone dies. A human life is lost and no amount of money, or any job, can ever replace the loss.

I was contemplating what other paths were open to me when I stepped into the hospital on Monday after Dr. Brown's death. I had purposely gone in early, so I could go to medical records and reread the charts of the people who had expired. I guess, hoping subconsciously, to figure out what went wrong and what we could have done differently. After reading many charts, I thought about Dr. Brown and all the various medical procedures, drugs, and machines we had used to save him.

I sat for a long time, thinking and wondering why we couldn't save more people. Why is it always the patients you come to love and work so hard to help, that seem to slip through your fingers?

I was so sad when I went into the unit that day that I said hello to no one. As I went to the heart monitors and got my little EKG strips to put in the charts, I felt empty. Then, Mae caught my eye and said there was some mail for me. I expected another one of the numerous hospital announcements or a nursing magazine.

Instead, I found your letter and pictures. I'm not ashamed to admit that I sat there and cried while I read the article about Jack Brown's life, his many contributions to the college, and the outpouring of love from faculty, staff, and students.

You mentioned in your letter that I once remarked that I only knew my patients as sick people. Dr. Brown was a man of great wit and personality. His warmth continued to shine through even as sick as he was. He was never once cross or hostile.

I can't begin to count the number of "ups" he gave me by just saying, "I'm glad you're here tonight" or the times you said how much the both of you had missed me when I was off duty. A few sparse words can water a desert. The two of you are a picture of pride.

He was dependent on you to help make him strong, and you did, and I, likewise, was dependent on the two of you to keep me going. I thrive on helping people and you both made me feel needed.

As I reread my wandering scribbles, I want to say thank you from deep inside. Your letter has shown me a new perspective and made me keep my profession. You have helped me realize the need to keep going even in the face of adversity and disappointment. Thank you, again..."

I treasure Sylvia's reflections and her friendship to this day. Perhaps it was just as well that she and Rainey were not there; saying goodbye would have been even more difficult. And I, no doubt, would have pumped both of them for answers, which they did not have.

Feeling like a lonely, homeless soul, I thanked Diane again and headed for the lobby and my waiting parents. Together we left the hospital behind forever. Not only had Jack died, but several years later, the hospital died, too; staff and equipment moved from the inner city to St. Louis County, and the old building site was demolished to make way for an apartment complex.

While my father went to fetch his car, I stood alone in the glare of the winter sun that reflected off the snow. It not only warmed my face, but my soul as well. I had been born under the astrology sign of Leo, and the sun was the root of my energy. With my eyes closed, I prayed that God's guidance and Jack's love would give me the grace and courage for whatever lay ahead. At that moment, I had the strangest feeling of detachment, as if I were looking out at the world through a one-way mirror. Over the next few days, I would become an observer, doing what was expected, without consciously participating.

By the time my parents and I arrived at the funeral home, the Valium had calmed my unhinged nerves. I had driven past Lupton's Funeral Home numerous times in my life. The entrance with its stately columns, circular drive, and abundance of foliage always made me think it was someone's great mansion, not a parlor for the deceased. A historic St. Louis landmark of colonial design, the massive white Georgian-style pillars extended two stories. On that day, the plants and bushes, weighted down by the heavy blanket of snow, could not be seen.

We were greeted by a uniformed doorman. I remember thinking that I should have put Jack's clothes in my leather brief case instead of in a brown paper bag. I felt as though we were entering a sacred place. The silence surrounding the antique furniture, oriental rugs, and long corridors leading nowhere, was daunting.

Because the doctors at the hospital were performing an

autopsy, which I had agreed to, it would be hours before Jack's body arrived at the funeral home. Although I wanted medical science to discover the cause of his death, I was unable to fathom the thought of Jack with his major organs removed.

The next two hours were haunting as I selected a casket and made arrangements for Jack's burial and final flight to Ohio. The place was like a gigantic warehouse; the sea of coffins was endless. There were hundreds of caskets: simple pine boxes, elegant bronze, solid mahogany, walnut, and cherry. In my state of shock, I expected a lid would fly open at any moment and some dead person might inquire, "What are you staring at?"

As my mother, dad, and I weaved among the caskets, we listened carefully to the undertaker as he gave his sales pitch, describing all the varieties and their prices. He was a tall stately gentleman in a dark suit, a pin-striped tie, and with a neatly trimmed white beard. He shared the staggering costs—many coffins were ten thousand dollars or more.

Understandably, I was unable to focus, so, without my father's assistance, I could not have made a selection. Although I wanted only the best for Jack, had my conservative father not been present, I might have been overly extravagant. After what seemed like hours, I finally selected a simple cherry wood casket. Jack loved beautiful wood.

I was confident that Lupton's would take care of all arrangements, so to sit and discuss the meticulous details was almost more than I could bear. I had slept not a wink the night before. As the undertaker's voice droned on, my eyelids kept closing, then they would open, and close again. I wanted to escape the oppressive atmosphere.

Not remembering the name of the New Concord funeral home, I told the funeral director that it was the only one in town. After contacting them, he called the airport and plans were made to fly Jack's body to Ohio on Saturday, two days hence. I would arrive in New Concord on Friday and go immediately to the mortuary to discuss details of the calling hours and funeral service.

After more than two long hours, my parents and I left the funeral home for the short drive to their apartment. It was too late for lunch and too early for dinner. It's all a blur, but I remember that I only wanted to sleep. I had to somehow escape the nightmare, but that was not to be. There were phone calls to be made, so I curled up on the sofa with my ear glued to the telephone, while my dear mother made ham and cheese sandwiches.

In spite of exhaustion, I had a mission. First, there were airline reservations to be made for my mother and me. My dad would drive to Ohio; he did not like to fly. Then, I called Bill and David. They had expected Jack to be released from the hospital, so there was shocked silence. They thought Jack was getting better. Hell, so did I. David would call Tony, Phil, and Barbara. Bill would call Maggie and ask her to put fresh sheets on all the beds and begin cleaning the house for the expected avalanche. Where was everyone going to sleep? I didn't know, but thought, we'll just have to worry about that tomorrow.

Then I called the dean of the college. It had been several days since we last communicated, so he was not expecting my tragic news. Momentarily, there was stillness on the line. After a brief description of the details, I said "Can we have a funeral service in Brown Chapel, Monday morning at 11 a.m.?" Response: "I'll make the arrangements." "Please tell Edwin Ahrens that Jack wants him to conduct the funeral service, and that I will call him tomorrow. Also, please tell Karla to notify board members immediately."

My next call was to Nora Abrams, "Jack died. Can you play his favorite, "Bach's Toccata and Fugue in D Minor?" Choking on her tears, she responded, "I'll do my best." Although Nora was acquainted with the piece, she had never played it before. I learned later that she spent the next three days at the organ in Brown Chapel.

At last the calls were complete. I was physically, mentally, and emotionally exhausted, but I had supper with my parents. What I ate escapes me, as does the conversation. My parents were in disbelief, as was I. We no doubt discussed mundane topics such as who was going to sleep where when all the family arrived in New Concord, and did I own the proper dress for a funeral? I did not have a suitable black dress. Whatever the occasion, my mother always expected me to be properly and elegantly dressed. When David and Bill picked us up at the airport the following morning, without question, we would have to stop at a Columbus department store.

Making a hasty retreat for the shower following dinner, I lit a cigarette before the open bathroom window, the winter cold freezing my naked body. My parents abhorred my smoking.

Alone at last, I cried buckets while I thought about Jack,

and wondered how I was going to survive. His love was powerful and enveloped my very being. I had lived at least three lifetimes already—my childhood into adulthood and two marriages. How in the world was I going to reinvent myself again?

Although I was beyond exhaustion, sleep did not come easy. Running in circles, my mind was unable to get off the treadmill. Nonetheless, to recline on a real bed for the first time in thirty days and, in my imagination, to feel Jack's arms engulf me, I was as close to heaven as I could get. Drifting off to sleep, I knew Jack would always be with me.

When I awoke, the stark reality of it all hit me like a stroke of lightening. I felt as if my life had shattered into a thousand pieces. I had slept for ten hours, but recovery from the ordeal would take months, if not years. It was like being poised on the age of a cliff, as if any minute I was going to fall into oblivion.

The brightly lit bathroom mirror reflected a haggard woman, ten pounds thinner and years older. I honestly didn't know how I was going to get through the day, much less the next week. I put on a stiff upper lip, held the tears at bay, and made my way to the kitchen. After hot coffee, poached eggs, and toast, my father drove my mother and me to Lambert airport for our flight to Columbus.

Walking into the airport was like returning to the nightmare of my arrival, when I had raced behind the gurney as paramedics rushed Jack to the ambulance. My mother and I slowly made our way to the last gate on the mile-long corridor.

The flight was noisy with the chatter of passengers. I closed my eyes, pretending to sleep. My mother tried to engage me in conversation. She was worried about this and that, but I was too broken-hearted to respond.

Arriving in Columbus late morning, I was overjoyed to see Bill and David, and rushed into their outstretched arms. I had almost forgotten what a good hug felt like. Their strong arms would be my security blanket in the days ahead. That morning, I clung to them both and held David until his tears subsided. Now, I was the only connection to his father. Bill was no longer a teenager; he had become a young man overnight. I was overjoyed to see him.

Knowing there would be time to share the devastation we all felt, I directed Bill to drive to my favorite dress shop. If I didn't buy a black dress at that moment, I knew it would never happen.

Luck was with me when I spotted a jet black wool knit with a cowl neckline, long sleeves, and a slightly flared skirt. Although it was a size smaller than I usually wore, it fit perfectly. I outgrew that dress many years ago, but I can still visualize it in my mind.

The details of our conversation as we drove home to New Concord, escape me, the words were no doubt endless, for we had been lost without each other. In the months ahead, Bill and David would be my supportive rocks. Little did I know that the cherished minutes in the car would be our last until the funeral was over and the last guest had departed.

As if I had been mesmerized by an out-of-body experience, for the next few days, I looked out at the world through my shattered eyes, and did what was expected. Consciously, I was not there. Although the calling hours, the funeral, and the grave side burial are foggy, the warmth and spirit of students and friends have lingered in my memory.

Reflecting on those days, I am reminded of Robert Browning's Pompelia when she said, "God stooping down gives us sufficient light in our darkness to rise by, and I rise." I know that my faith in God gave me the courage and the grace to rise up and do what was necessary.

"Death is not extinguishing the light;
it is putting out the lamp because dawn has come."
—Rabindranath Tagore

THE TRANSFORMATION

*"Inside myself is a place where I live all alone, and
that's where you renew your springs that never dry up."*
–Pearl S. Buck

Bill graduated from John Glenn High School in June and we moved to the country. The feeling was akin to leaving a part of my life behind. Although it was a sweeping change, it was not as torturous as it might have been earlier in the spring. We were only transplanted six miles, so our friends would be close by. Nevertheless, moving day had its nostalgic, tearful moments as I relived life with Jack at that special college. With David's and Katie's help, Bill and I packed our belongings in a rental truck and traveled the gravel road to what would forever be our country cottage.

Surrounded by the sounds of nature with its gentle summer breezes and rustling pastures, occasionally interrupted by the crowing of a rooster, singing birds, or mooing cows, the fresh country air was therapeutic and enabled me to think and meditate for hours on end. Although I had my son and a place to live, I often felt wounded and abandoned like a lost, lonely animal. Some days, I missed Jack so much that getting up in the morning was my only accomplishment.

Now and then, time stopped as I reclined in the tall grass with the sun beating on my skin. Our pets, Charlie and Patrick snuggled nearby. Staring into nothingness, I pondered my future without Jack. I wondered where he was, and whose body his spirit might have entered. Being alone with my own thoughts became vital to my healing. As Pearl Buck once said, "Inside myself is a place where I live all alone, and that's where you renew your springs that never dry up."

With Jack as my partner, I had blossomed beyond my wildest expectations. Years later, I asked myself, "How many women at age forty-four are free to pursue their dreams without any barriers in their path?" What a gift and what a legacy Jack left me.

When Jack died, our story-and-a-half Williamsburg replica was covered with its roof and siding, the chimney, with its seven thousand bricks, was in place, and the windows had been installed. We had selected authentic Williamsburg paints: chocolate brown for the doors and shutters, and the window and door trim was a dark grey, as was the molding under the eaves.

The Cottage

Typical of early Virginia architecture, the molding consisted of three-inch-square blocks of wood spaced an inch apart across the entire roof line, on the front and back of the house. While the trim and shutters had been primed and painted, they needed a second coat. Standing on the ladder in the hot summer sun, I daydreamed about Jack as the paint flowed from the brush and perspiration seeped from my pores. Bill worked that summer for an oil well company, so painting alone was not an easy chore.

The interior of the cottage had been finished the previous summer. The walls were an eggshell white and the woodwork a Williamsburg blue/green. The cherry wood flooring came from a one hundred-year-old house in New Concord. Prior to moving day, a scarlet red carpet was laid on the stairwell and throughout the two bedrooms on the second floor. There were three dormer windows that looked westward over our hayfield.

My bedroom had a small fireplace adorned with antique

wrought iron trim that had originally come from Jack's parents' home. Furnishings included a four poster bed, purchased from our neighbor, Al Johnson, and an antique chest of drawers that we had brought back from Maine.

It was a warm, comfortable room. I laid a fire one evening, stretched out on the floor, and closed my eyes. Jack was there; I could almost feel his presence. How he had loved watching our little house take shape. It was like having our own cottage in the Cotswolds of rural England.

Cozy and charming, the first floor was a great room with a walk-in fireplace, complete with crane and black soup kettle; a small den with book shelves and the only sliding door closet in the house; a bathroom with pinewood fixtures and shower stall; and a postage stamp kitchen with a pantry under the stairwell. Though small, it was functional.

Had Jack and I known the house was to be a permanent residence, we surely would have planned a larger kitchen. On one wall, the stainless steel sink was set in a rough hewn pine cabinet with a countertop-high refrigerator just adjacent. The only working space was the top of an antique bureau. In the corner sat a portable washing machine. Clothes were dried the old fashioned way, on a clothesline. To this day, I fantasize about the fragrant aroma of bed sheets hung to dry out-of-doors.

Except for the furnishings in the great room and den, most of our furniture was in storage. My two Chippendale love seats faced each other in front of the fireplace. A drop-leaf cherry dining table and chairs, where Bill and I talked for hours, graced the east window. Opposite the fireplace, my pecan wood hutch almost overpowered the room. In a far corner sat an antique pine doughboy. Early settlers placed their bread dough to rise in its deep hollow interior, but I used it for storage.

Other than the house and the barn, the only structure not in the original plans was a two-car garage painted Williamsburg cream, the same as the main house. The extra storage space was a necessity to house Bill's 1960 vintage MGB, a full-size refrigerator, lawnmower, and power saw for wood-cutting. Although the house had electric baseboard heating, a wood-burning fire was preferable on chilly fall evenings and even on rainy summer days.

As the summer wore on, Bill and I slowly began to get on with living. No longer was Bill only my son, he had become a young adult, and my best friend. Long, heart-wrenching conversations, sometimes with tears flowing, often took place over breakfast. On one such morning, I remember a gentle breeze wafted in the windows, and we talked so long that my butt felt like it was glued to the chair.

Topics were numerous; everything from what kind of job Bill might find until he went to college, his feelings about his dad's and my divorce, how much he had come to admire and respect Jack, Bill's girl friends, past and present, and the continuing ever present question, what was I going to do with my life?

One of my favorite actresses, Katharine Hepburn, once said, "Life is to be lived. If you have to support yourself, you had bloody well better find some way that is going to be interesting. And you don't do that by sitting around wondering about yourself." Difficult as it was going to be, I knew it was time to shift gears and get moving.

Without much soul searching, I declined Garrison's and Peter's urgings to move to the nation's capitol. There was a director of admissions position opening at a small college in the Washington area, and Garrison urged me to apply. Having explored the corridors and interviewed guidance counselors and students at more high schools than I cared to remember, I did not want to be a director of admissions ever again. Although Peter had invited me to live at his home, the thought of living in Washington did not fill my heart with palpitations.

Furthermore, I now owned my own place which required my attention. I was deeply grateful for their care and concern, but the time had arrived to forge my own way.

Since early spring, my mind had been exploring the possibility of graduate school–a lifelong ambition. Although I needed to allocate resources carefully, there were sufficient funds until I completed a master's degree. Having concluded I wanted to continue my journey in the academic community, I opted to pursue a degree in higher education administration.

The toughest part was the Graduate Record Exam. I had not taken any kind of test in over twenty years, so I was somewhat apprehensive. Needless to say, I was overjoyed when I passed first time around.

Immediately, I made application to The Ohio State University for the fall term, while Bill's job with the oil well company continued. His days were unusually long, from sunrise to sunset six days a week. It was back-breaking work, but the pay enabled him to purchase a new truck before he went to college the following January. When he wasn't working, he was sleeping.

Bill and I didn't see much of each other that summer and fall, but there were endless chores to keep me busy and divert the misery of my mind. There was painting to be done, grass to mow, flowers, tomatoes, and strawberries to be planted, and horses to be fed, groomed, and watered.

Our mare had survived the cold winter, and foaled in early June. What an unforgettable and exciting day. I awakened shortly after the sun came up, and was having my morning coffee while listening to the radio. A hot, steamy day, the temperature was seventy-five degrees and it was only eight o'clock.

I was preparing to head for the barn and give Echo her morning feed when, suddenly, bleary-eyed Bill, dressed in jeans and no shirt, came bounding down the stairs. "What is that noise?" he said. I replied, "What noise?" as I turned the radio off. A desperate-sounding scream was coming from somewhere west of the house. Bill opened the front door and ran to the far edge of the lawn. He could see two distinct brown silhouettes in the far corner of our property. "Echo has foaled," he yelled.

Running back into the house, Bill was up the stairs, three at a time. He slipped on his high top basketball shoes and literally flew down the stairs and through the open front door. He raced as fast as his legs could carry him through the three-foot-high hayfield.

He found the newborn foal trapped in a three-trunk tree. Her head was twisted in the barbed-wire fence, and her neck was bleeding. She struggled to free herself, while Bill hugged her with the hope of preventing further injury.

Although I had started out right behind Bill, there was no keeping up with my long-legged son. In an anxious voice, he hollered for me to get the wire cutters, a halter, and lead rope from the barn. By the time I returned from the half-mile stint, my pulse was racing and I was short of breath.

Meanwhile, Echo, panting and snorting heavily, had worked herself into a fit as she raced back and forth along the fence row. Bill told me later he was concerned that Echo might jump the fence to reach her newborn. Bill asked me to open the gate, and I let the mare out into the hayfield. She was so upset that I was afraid she might run off.

Bill reassured me she wouldn't go anywhere as long as her

foal was there. Once outside the fence, where she could see her offspring, Echo settled down. With Echo and me looking on, Bill carefully cut the wire, avoiding further harm to the foal.

When the last wire was snipped, the young Arabian hopped from the middle of the three-trunk tree and bounced like a deer to her mother. Together, mother and daughter pranced around until Bill was able to get the halter on the newborn. Then, we led the horses to the barn.

Echo and *Yasmin*

Later on that day, the foal came looking for Bill–they had bonded. With a white star on her forehead and a rich auburn coat, she carried her head proudly, her tail flowed in the breeze, and her long spindly legs raced around as she explored her new environment.

Amazingly, she had only three or four small scrapes on her neck. As if I had just given birth, she was a joy to behold. We named her Yasmin, the Arabian name for jasmine, the flower. How I wished Jack could have been there that day. He would have loved her. His spirit was, no doubt, looking on.

With two horses to feed, the need for grain and hay multiplied. Monthly, I went to New Concord's feed mill to purchase two thirty-pound sacks of grain. Sufficient hay grew on our property to feed Echo and Yasmin, as well as our neighbor's two cows.

Steve and his wife, Jeanette, and their two girls, ages six and eight, lived in a trailer on their small plot of land. Eventually, they built a three bedroom ranch, doing most of the work themselves. Together, they saved my life on many occasions, particularly in the winter when snow needed to be plowed, or when I was away. They were always there to feed and water the horses. I don't know what I would have done without them.

Jeanette was not your typical farmer's wife. In her late twenties, with flowing red hair and a voluptuous body, she paraded around the countryside in her skimpy shorts and halter top, leaving little to the imagination. A hard working young woman, Jeanette mowed her grass, tilled the garden, and raised fresh vegetables to feed her family.

She was an inspiration to me. My garden was pint-size in comparison. That first summer, I was determined to grow tomatoes and strawberries. Having grown one or two tomato plants in my previous life, this time I expanded my vision to twenty-five plants. With an overabundance of sun and rain, the tomatoes multiplied beyond my expectations. I couldn't pick or eat them fast enough. By September, we were overrun and I was giving tomatoes away.

I also had planted a twelve-foot flower bed, which Bill surrounded with railroad ties. As one turned into the gravel drive, the yellow daffodils, red roses, and pink and purple zinnias shone brilliantly in the sun with the gigantic chimney for a backdrop.

Difficult as my changing life was that summer, taking care of the house and the property was an additional challenge. For the first time in three years, I was faced with cleaning house, doing laundry, and washing dishes. There was no room for even a portable dishwasher.

Maggie had spoiled me. Though she lived in the nearby village of Norwich, I missed her. She was not only a friend, but an important member of our family. Maggie continued to work for the college, but she did help me clean a few times that first summer. As time went on, and Bill went off to college, I could not justify having a cleaning lady for such a small house.

Moreover, physical labor became an important component in getting my life back together. Work made me feel good. It gave me a sense of accomplishment and took my mind away from the loneliness.

Whether I was working inside or out, I communed with nature, with God, and, yes, with Jack's spirit. It was like I had returned to the earth's natural elements for light, sustenance, and healing. Often I derived great satisfaction from meditating as I sat on the back steps or walked in the woods—more so than if I had gone to church. I knew God was with me wherever I was.

As I reflected on the palette of my early life, I thought about my love of nature, the out-of-doors, and growing up in a small town. As a teenager, I had mowed the grass, worked in my mother's iris bed, walked with my girlfriends in the neighborhood creek bed, road my bicycle to school, and read books under the covers with a flashlight.

Summers were spent canoeing, swimming, eating s'mores, and singing around the fire at Girl Scout camp. Summers also meant fireflies, mumbly peg, kick the can, slumber parties, and watching the gallantry of horses at the county fair. There was even a neighbor's horse to pet over the back fence.

What goes around comes around; now I had horses of my own—childhood fantasies do come true. The robust aroma of Echo and Yasmin, the freshly cut hay, and the mineral-filled feed gave my olfactory nerves new sensations.

Occasionally, there was the whiff of an offensive order, the sign a skunk was in the vicinity. I remember that our dog, Patrick, occasionally tangled with a skunk. The stench was unbearable. We soon learned the only cure was tomato juice. Shaking to dry himself, Patrick sprayed juice everywhere. Skunks, possums hiding in the barn, an occasional snake, and Charlie's mice were a few of the lesser joys of country living.

One evening when Garrison and his wife were visiting, I hosted a party for a number of friends who were attending a Muskingum board meeting. Charlie was outside, meowing, so one of my guests opened the door to let her in. Someone screamed as Charlie proudly displayed her catch, a live mouse dangled from her mouth. I grabbed a broom and quickly ushered her out the door.

When I wasn't taking care of the animals or working around the property, I was immersed in my lifelong passion with books. After several months I rediscovered *The Thornbirds*, finally finishing it. Then I turned to novels such as *A Woman of Substance* and *A Woman of Independent Means*. They helped me escape the pain. Self-help and devotional books, along with Catherine Marshall, Norman Vincent Peale, and other religious authors, also gave me hope and inspiration, and brought peace to my wilted spirit.

A friend recommended a little book entitled, *How to Survive the Loss of a Love* by Melba Colgrove, Harold H. Bloomfield, and Peter McWilliams. As its poetry and philosophy talked about sticking to the sidewalk and other insane ideas, it sent me into bouts of laughter on the one hand, and on the other, the tears flowed like water. This wonderful book, in its simple format, enabled me to cope with the loss, the pain, the healing, and the surviving.

I had suffered loss before with the ending of relationships, the death of my brother, and the demise of my first marriage, but I had never before endured a loss which totally depleted my strength. Like an hour glass turned upside down, I was completely drained.

Pampering myself, I sometimes napped during the day, while the nights were restless and tormented with bad dreams. Saturday nights were the worst. Fortunately, Bill was usually home on Sundays; otherwise, it would have been unbearable.

Some weekends we spent time with David and Katie, or with our good friends, the Abrams, who often stopped to visit or we joined them at their nearby farm for a cookout. The Abrams' son, Craig, and daughter, Jane, were Bill's high school classmates.

Occasionally, I dined with Jack's assistant, Gay Whitaker, and her husband, Reeb. Concert pianists of Carnegie Hall caliber, they chose, instead, the stage of Muskingum College. Gay idolized Jack, and had difficulty with his death–she loved him almost as much as we did.

Upon reflection, the summer of 1978 was a period of transition, like being suspended on a bridge between one world and the next. It was a first step on the road to my new life.

Thinking about those long ago days, I'm puzzled. Why didn't I write in my journal? Perhaps, it would have been too painful to put my feelings on paper. It was too soon to relive what I had written while Jack was dying. I should have been dealing with my feelings, but my nervous energy kept me occupied. I remember thinking, "Some day I will write a book about my thirty day journey in the ICU, but not now."

Perhaps the healing process would have progressed at a faster clip if I had put pen to paper, letting my emotions flow, instead of letting them churn in turmoil. The next time I'm faced with a catastrophic loss, I will be sure to put my innermost thoughts on paper. Writing can be like having a companion through difficult times.

Bridging the gap between my old life and the new lasted several years. I wish God had given me a road map to my next destination. Some days were bumpy, consumed with roadblocks, and sometimes there were no guard rails. Like taking two steps forward and one back, I made the wrong turn or ran out of steam; one day, I ran out of gas on the freeway and got my first speeding ticket, as well.

Occasionally, I just sat down and had a good cry. Other times, there was smooth sailing, albeit too fast, and then my impatience often led to mistakes. Fortunately, I averted any major disasters.

Until that summer, my life had been predetermined according to the schedule outlined in my appointment book. Everything proceeded according to a vertical hierarchy of meetings, luncheons, and activities from morning until late evening.

Moving to the country, the pattern of my days took on a horizontal look. Time and activities were insignificant compared to the value of working in the garden, staring into space as the setting sun went over the hill, or simply walking in the woods, filling a brown paper bag with morel mushrooms. The cone-shaped delicacies, sautéed in butter, are among God's most succulent vegetables. But those private moments would become fewer and fewer.

The cottage continued to be my haven, but when autumn came I was on the road three days a week to The Ohio State University. I sold my gas guzzling Ford Granada, and purchased the newly imported Ford Fiesta, which had front wheel drive. Muskingum's board chair, Philip Caldwell, had played a primary role in bringing the Fiesta to the United States. Needless to say, the satisfaction I derived from purchasing my first car enhanced my sense of independence.

One day, driving home from class, I remember thinking, "Not a single soul knows where I am." Feeling safe, secure, and completely capable of managing whatever might come my way, the hour-and-a-half drive each way to Columbus didn't seem long at all.

On the other hand, navigating my way around The Ohio State University campus was like walking in circles through a maze in an English garden. You never knew when you might encounter a dead end.

It was a strange feeling to be out in the world again. Initially, I was intimidated by the immense size of the campus. Once I learned my way around, and discovered most of my graduate classes were comprised of only twenty-five students, I began to feel more comfortable.

Many of my classmates were working towards a Ph.D., while I was in the Master's program. I enrolled in four courses each of the fall and spring quarters for the next two years. The most enjoyable and motivational class focused on leadership, management, and writing as they related to proposal development. This course was also utilized by students writing their dissertations.

I had done some volunteer work with the Ohio College Association, an organization representing private college presidents. When the staff learned of my interest in proposal development, they asked me to write a grant request to the National Endowment for the Humanities. Regrettably, the project was not funded, but I gained a great deal of experience. In addition, I was able to secure a five thousand dollar corporate gift, my first major philanthropic donor.

The only unpleasant graduate school experience took place in my last quarter, when I took a course in the School of Business along with two hundred-and-fifty other students. The professor from India spoke very little English and was difficult to understand. Several times, I made an appointment for assistance; he never showed at the scheduled hour. Since I did not need the credit to complete my degree, I dropped out after several agonizing weeks. I certainly wasn't going to flunk the course and ruin my 3.5 grade point average.

Coming out of my shell and relating to people again was highly motivating. Suddenly, I felt alive, and learning became more exciting than it had ever been. I loved every minute.

During this phase, I studied long hours and wrote volumes of papers. A collaborative research paper was published. Although my little cottage was the perfect place for study, I also spent long hours in reading and research at the OSU library. When I was on campus, the library was my home.

When it came time for Thanksgiving and Christmas, I took a break from the academic world. The thought of holiday celebrations filled my heart with feelings of dread. How, I thought, would I ever get through them without Jack?

Bill and I went to St. Louis for Thanksgiving, where we spent time with my parents, and Bill saw his dad. Not being able to bear the thought of Christmas at the cottage, I purchased four airplane tickets to San Diego, and Bill, David, Katie, and I spent the holidays with David's brother, Phil, and his family. Although holidays would be dreadful for many years, traveling that year to a warmer climate was a blessing. Had it not been for Phil and Becky's children, Callie and Tyler, it would have been a year without Christmas.

During the second quarter at OSU, I became friends with

one of my professors. Sophie was a single, divorced mother with four grown children. Petite, with deep auburn, curly hair, dancing brown eyes, and freckles, Sophie radiated flair and style in everything she did. She was relaxed and confident—a role model that I needed at the time.

Both of us had lost husbands, and neither of us knew many people in Columbus. She was from Ann Arbor, Michigan. We often enjoyed dinner together. Although Sophie had a steady boyfriend who lived in Michigan, she was looking for new male companionship.

She occasionally invited me to parties at her home with faculty friends and other adult students. It was a fun time, but I always felt uncomfortable. Relearning how to meet single men socially at the age of forty-three was difficult, to say the least. Although Sophie offered to introduce me to several of her male friends, I declined. It was too soon.

Sophie lived in a small, but lovely Cape Cod in Clintonville. Some evenings after class, she and I dined at a nearby restaurant. Occasionally, I stayed all night at her place, and went to class the next day before driving home. One such occasion evokes strong images.

The time was late February or early March. Bill had enrolled at Miami University in Oxford in January, so I was foot-loose and fancy-free. Snow began to fall in late afternoon, and Sophie invited me to stay all night. Morning arrived and it was still snowing. I had been gone from home almost twenty-four hours, so I was anxious to head for the hills to feed my animals.

The trip took almost three hours, double the usual time, and the snow never stopped. When I reached my driveway, the horses instantly recognized the car and raced along the fence row, neighing to greet me.

What a welcome committee they were, along with Patrick and Charlie. I was amazed that not an accident was to be found anywhere in the house. Charlie had her litter box, but I was concerned about Patrick who had not been outside since the previous afternoon.

I was exhausted after the intense drive, but there was no rest until the animals were fed, watered, and firewood had been carried to the hearth. I changed into old jeans, my warmest coat, and riding boots (a birthday gift from Bill) and trudged off to the barn in knee-deep snow.

My thousand-pound pets were so excited at the thought of food that they almost ran over me in their glee. Once I'd scooped the feed out of the barrel and into their troughs, all you could hear was the quiet, rapid chopping of their teeth.

Leaving the horses to their grain and hay, I took a shovel and broke the ice in the water trough so that Echo and Yasmin could have something to drink. Then, I carried an armload of firewood into the cottage.

After several trips through the whirling snow with enough wood to last until evening, I was able to shed my snow-covered coat, warm some soup on the stove, and lay a fire. By then, it was after three o'clock in the afternoon and I was ready to collapse. Moreover, I was anxious to start reading my new book.

At the OSU bookstore the previous day, I had purchased Lauren Bacall's recently released book, *By Myself,* a memoir about her acting career and love affair with Humphrey Bogart. I could hardly wait to read her story. An incredible romantic, I related to her life with Bogie, and her devastation when he died of cancer.

On that cold winter afternoon, with a blizzard blowing around my cottage and a fire blazing on the hearth, I kicked off my boots and curled up on a love seat with my book and a mug of steaming vegetable soup. Just before dark, I made another trip to the barn to feed the horses, and brought in enough firewood to last until morning.

Except for the snorting of the horses, an eerie, ghostly quiet hung in the atmosphere. The full moon shone brightly on the fluffy white blanket covering the landscape. I remember feeling Jack's presence and thinking maybe he was one of those stars twinkling in the heavens. I took a deep breath and my nostrils sniffed the frosty night air.

Returning to the house and locking the door, I felt warm and secure, as if I were a bunny rabbit burrowing in its home for the winter. The doors had only single locks, and the windows were without shades or curtains, as in Williamsburg, but I felt amazingly safe and relished the privacy. I was confident that God was looking after me. I also had my dog, my cat, and my book for comfort.

After throwing more wood on the fire, I fixed a gin martini on the rocks and settled in with Lauren, Bogie, and their friends. The book was filled with anecdotes about some of my favorite actors, including Katharine Hepburn, Spencer Tracy, David Niven,

Frank Sinatra, and numerous others. Enthralled by the story, I don't remember when I had dinner, or what I ate. With Bill no longer around, I didn't do much cooking, so I often enjoyed one of Stouffer's Lean Cuisines®.

Except for the crackling fire, silence reigned. The phone never rang. In all my days, I had never devoured a three hundred and seventy-five page book in one sitting. I had been so hungry to relate to someone my age whose husband was several decades older, and who also had lost her husband. I was captivated by Lauren and Bogie's story, and would eventually reread many chapters. I also learned a few things which helped me along the road to recovery.

First, I was grateful that Jack had died in the hospital, and not in our bed. I might not have been able to sleep at all with the terrible recollections that accompany critical illness. Secondly, I learned one shouldn't change their environment too quickly. And, thirdly, I concluded it would be disastrous to jump into a new relationship too soon. Bacall had an unsettling experience with Frank Sinatra, which not only ended the romantic encounter, but concluded the friendship. Years went by before they spoke again.

In my own case, I was shocked by several male acquaintances that were married and wanted to console me. They thought it might be nice if we had a sexual encounter. Whatever gave them the idea I wanted to be intimate with them? I was amused and remember laughing to myself at their audacity.

Having heard similar stories from others, I wonder if men want to experience what the deceased may have enjoyed, or do they just think the widow must be hungry for sex and would be an easy lay? Whatever, it is a sad commentary on the fate of women and men at a time when they are struggling with their grief.

One of Bacall's friends, who had previously lost his wife, said to her "You'll never forget Bogie; nor would you want to. You'll just one day be able to put him in a different place in your life." What a powerful message. I've never forgotten it.

Many years passed before I put Jack Brown in the proper perspective, but I eventually came to understand that our time together was not meant to last a lifetime. From Jack, I learned many things. He taught me how to love, to live life to the fullest each and every minute, to work hard, to take risks, and most importantly, to believe in myself. Then, he sent me on my way to see what I could do.

What a gift, and what an unforgettable day reading Bacall's story. Between chapters, I put another log on the fire, went to the bathroom, or put on a pot of coffee. By the time I came to the final page, the last log had disintegrated and it was after two o'clock in the morning. I let Patrick out one last time, awaited his return, turned out the lights, and cuddled Charlie in my arms as we ascended the stairs.

The brilliant moon flooded the bedroom as I drifted off to sleep with Charlie curled at my feet. Too exhausted to dream, I slept soundly until after nine the next morning.

Upon awakening, my eyes were blinded by the sun's rays reflected off the layer of fresh snow. I put on my jeans and a heavy sweater, and moseyed to the kitchen to brew the coffee. Looking through the paned window, I peered at Echo and Yasmin as they hovered at the fence. I opened the door and they greeted me with their usual snorting. My customary ritual was to trudge to the barn and feed the horses while the coffee perked.

When I returned to the house, I turned on the radio for news, weather, and music. I didn't have to drive to Columbus for class that day, for which I was grateful. Besides, the news reports indicated a foot or more of snow had fallen overnight. An avalanche had blanketed the countryside. Except for making a few phone calls and seeing an occasional neighbor, I was isolated from the world for several days.

Wrapped in my cocoon and sheltered from the storm, I reread passages of Bacall's book, wrote a letter to my parents, called my son, and worked on a research paper. The solitude renewed my energy, gave me time for reflection, and time to continue pondering my future without Jack. It was still difficult to imagine. He had become so integral to every fiber of my being.

As I contemplated and meditated, I recalled Jack's chats with Albert Johnson, the wood carver and farmer who lived across the road. Our fourteen acres had originally been part of Albert's farm. He had lived in his house for more than seventy years, and knew the local folklore and neighbors for miles around. Albert could not believe that a college president would sit on the steps and pass the time of day with him.

For Jack, Albert's stories were a history lesson. As a young man, he had crafted a pine cupboard from trees on the property. His legacy lives on, for that china cabinet stands today in my son's dining room. The summer following Jack's death, Albert, a widower, remarried and moved to his bride's home, three miles away.

He sold his property to the Barney family. Mack, the eldest son, managed the property, raised some cattle, and worked on a highway construction crew. Normally, I didn't see much of Mack, but the day after the snow storm, he and neighbor Steve came to my rescue. They plowed and shoveled our long driveway. With his tractor, Steve also cleared the snow blocking the other properties on Peach Lane. Both men were hard workers, and I was grateful to have them as friends and neighbors.

The following spring Mack's dog, part spaniel, would give birth to a litter of ten puppies. Much to our surprise, Mack gave Bill one of the dogs, partly to ease the pain of losing our beloved Patrick. Regrettably, when I was out-of-town, Patrick wandered from home and was attacked by some wild dogs. To this day, I have guilt feelings about my negligence. We buried Patrick on the property and welcomed Bo, our new black spaniel, who would accompany his master to college and live to the ripe old age of fourteen.

Bill, Bo, and Nancy

As I reminisce about those long-ago days, there were many exceptional people. Getting my life back together without them would not have been nearly as unforgettable. Like glue binding two pieces of wood, it was my friends who sustained me.

One winter Sunday afternoon, an OSU classmate drove to the country to have dinner with me. His name was Andy. Developing a new relationship was an awkward and uncomfortable feeling. I was almost forty-five years old and I didn't know how to be or how to act. It was like being a shy teenager all over again, except my heart just wasn't in it; a piece had broken off and died with Jack.

Andy was a former Marine, and a fun-loving bachelor, twelve years younger than Yours Truly. Trim at five-foot-ten with brown hair, a neatly trimmed mustache, and questioning, distant gray/green eyes, Andy never seemed quite sure of what he wanted at any given moment. And, furthermore, I think he didn't quite know what to make of me. He probably was just as uncomfortable as I was.

When Andy arrived, we toured the snow-covered property and then, before dinner and on the spur of the moment, I suggested we go sledding. Andy was ecstatic and, for a brief moment, I felt like a sixteen-year-old embarking on a new adventure. I had not been sledding since Bill was a boy.

For the next hour, we laughed and joked as we traversed up and down a neighbor's steep hill, occasionally tumbling off the sled and rolling in the snow. It was a fun time. With frost bitten fingers and toes, we finally headed to the house to grill steaks in the fireplace. Andy carried in additional firewood, and we settled in to sip wine, savor the t-bones, and chat before he left for Columbus.

After his departure, much to my surprise, I found myself treasuring the warmth of a new friend. Slowly, but surely, some joy had re-entered my life. I suddenly realized I would survive the nightmare after all. But, it would be on my own and without Andy.

We saw each other again on several occasions, and in class, but our relationship was short-lived when he learned I had a twenty-year-old son. When Andy kissed me, I was not enamored with his style or his mustache, so his exit was just as well.

While friends, old and new, would forever weave in and out of my life, I have treasured those who stood beside me and inspired me during my transformation from one life to the next. Their caring friendship and God's sunlight continued to guide my way.

One hot, sun-drenched morning in the summer of 1980, the telephone rang at my little cottage. A deep, masculine voice asked, "Is this Nancy Brown?" Yes, I replied. "You don't know me, but my name is Harvey Stegemoeller and I am the president of Capital University in Columbus, Ohio." I gulped and took a deep breath before saying "hello" or "good morning," or whatever I said.

Upon receiving my degree from The Ohio State University

in June of that year, I had circulated my resume to friends and educators. Obviously, someone had sent Dr. Stegemoeller my resume. Needless to say, I was excited to think my credentials were of interest to someone.

Traveling to and from Columbus in my yellow Ford Fiesta, I met with President Stegemoeller several times over the summer. New to Capital University, he had just concluded his first year as president. He was also an ordained Lutheran pastor, and father of six children. Harvey, as everyone called him, was a warm, sensitive man with a keen wit, inquiring mind, and a native Texan drawl. Over three hour-long meetings we shared our backgrounds, interests, and aspirations.

Harvey, I would soon learn, was a master-mind when it came to finances. The university's board of trustees had given him a challenge: to erase the university's million dollar deficit, and to increase the enrollment. He was looking for someone to help him raise money and reverse the budget decline.

Certainly, I was flattered that Dr. Stegemoeller thought my background and experience qualified me for the job. He said that he was impressed with my administrative experience, and with the way in which I had gotten my life back together after Jack's death.

Although I was seeking to be an assistant to a college president, rather than a fund raiser, he was faced with a budgetary crisis and could not justify hiring an assistant. Finally, he convinced me that I was the ideal person to be his director of special projects. I would be responsible for initiating contact with corporations and private foundations, working with faculty on their projects, and using my research and writing skills to create successful grant proposals.

And so, on October 1, 1980, I launched my new life at Capital University, the most exciting and rewarding opportunity of my career. Once again, I was *Standing in the Sun* as another journey unfolded. I would forever treasure Jack's love, his legacy, and the memories of the cottage where I created my new world. Like forming a multi-layered sandwich, another layer to my life was about to begin.

"Life is to be lived. If you have to support yourself, you had bloody well better find some way that is going to be interesting. And you don't do that by sitting around wondering about yourself."

—*Katharine Hepburn*

EPILOGUE

"...the great symphony of life goes on—with one unwavering purpose—to create what is to be..."
—Gwen Frostic

My new life began, and what had been a nightmare faded in the distance, like in a dream.

The crisp, fall morning I started my new job with Capital University will remain forever in my memory. When I arrived at the administrative offices, President Stegemoeller was waiting to escort me to my new abode. Except for a bank of file cabinets, the only furniture was a desk, piled high with correspondence, and an armless chair. The room was windowless, musty, and sterile, as if no one had lived there for a long time.

Completely covered with three-foot stacks of letters and envelopes, the desk was not visible that first morning. "You might want to begin by going through those papers—there may be money hidden there," Dr. Stegemoeller chuckled. The office had been vacant for two years, and secretaries had stacked the mail and never opened an envelope.

After a coat of sunrise yellow paint, a clean carpet, and artwork reflecting my favorite impressionist painters, the space became my home away from home for the next nineteen years.

The initial weeks were spent clearing the desk, reading files, and getting acquainted with fellow staff members. Not a dollar was to be found among the hundreds of letters and envelopes. Any plans or reports from my predecessor were skimpy, at best.

Obviously, the challenge was to create my own job, somewhat like laying track for a new railroad, and unsure of its final destination. I would come to learn by doing—one day at a time. The better part of a year had passed before I felt knowledgeable about the university. Most lunch hours were spent getting acquainted with the Columbus community, or table hopping with faculty in order to learn who had projects in need of funding.

Raising money during my first five years at Capital University was not easy. There was an operating deficit, and outside support from previous donors trickled in small amounts. For the most part, corporations and foundations did not support organizations that were in arrears.

As I recollect, my first grant was for ten thousand dollars.

I thought that was a lot of money at the time. Years later, when seeking six-and-seven-figure gifts, ten thousand seemed minuscule in comparison.

While raising dollars was complex, the research, the cultivation of prospects, and the writing of grant proposals was a time-consuming and labor intensive process. I loved it; it was my forte. Much more than asking for dollars, it was the thrill of making things happen, working with faculty and staff to design creative projects for the education of students.

Sometimes, the planning and writing of a grant was complicated with numerous faculty involved. The creation of a major project often took the better part of a year, with many drafts, and other times, a proposal was crafted in less than a week, or sometimes in one day. My writing companions were a stack of yellow legal pads and a box of Number 2 pencils.

Even after technology arrived, it took me several years before I could write without a pencil. To this day, I am more creative with a pen in hand.

Research, planning, cultivating prospects, soliciting donors, and then writing the proposal became an exciting way of life. I worked for two incredible college presidents, Harvey Stegemoeller and Josiah H. Blackmore, from whom I learned many things. They were each unique in their own way; they were fun to take on calls, and they permitted me to be their ghost writer. I could not have been more flattered.

The Capital University community embraced me with warmth and friendship, and I felt as though I had been adopted by a new family. I thrived on my job, new friends and colleagues, basketball and football games, music and theater events, alumni gatherings, et cetera. My new friends often teased me about having allegiance to another college.

I may have left Muskingum, but the place would never leave my heart. When Muskingum played Capital in sporting events, I would spend half the game with my Muskie friends and then move to Capital's side of the gym or football field. Had it not been for the Capital community, the CAP family, those first few years in Columbus would have been lonely indeed.

Moving from the country to the big city, I barely knew a soul, with the exception of a few Muskingum board members who entertained me from time to time. My friend, Sophia, from Ohio State moved back to Michigan, and I missed her.

While I treasured my old friends, I knew it was time to move on. Friends-to-come would be an eclectic group from diverse backgrounds and cultures. Penny Kean, a statuesque, olive-skinned woman, lived in my apartment complex, a predominantly Jewish community. We became friends. She, too, had lost her husband, and had two college age children.

I had lived my early childhood in the Jewish community of St. Louis. I felt as if I had come home. For two years, Penny and I dined together almost every Friday, and midweek we often went to a restaurant in our neighborhood where we knew the pianist.

Eliza was not only a talented musician, but she was a matchmaker, par excellence. Men and women, young and old, came to sing with Eliza. She knew them all, including their family history.

I particularly recall a singer, reminiscent of Frank Sinatra. We dated a few times, and he came to my fiftieth birthday celebration. There was another person—a crazy but loveable older man whose mother had taught piano at Capital. I quietly turned away from his persistence. Then, there was the guy, recently divorced, who always wore a Hawaiian shirt. He cooked dinner for me one evening in my apartment. One date was enough.

I remember a handsome, well-dressed man with dark ebony skin and a voice like Nat King Cole. He invited Penny and me to dinner one evening. Brian, a sales representative with a highly respected corporation, picked us up in his Lincoln convertible. Later, he asked if I would consider dating him. I was flattered, but without a moment's hesitation, I said, "I don't think that would be a good idea." He seemed to understand and appreciated my honesty. Why I didn't give it a try, I wondered later; he might have been fun. On the other hand, it was just as well left alone. My son and my parents would never have understood.

Then, there was a divorced biology professor, father of four children, who dated a variety of women, but eventually married a longtime colleague. We worked together on some grant projects and, after I had surgery, he surprised me by bringing dinner to my apartment one evening.

That is a brief sampling of male friends during my early years in Columbus. For the most part, the men and I were from different cuts of cloth, and many were in search of twenty-five-year-olds— which I was not. Those with whom I did have something in common were either married, or were dating a different woman every night.

As if I were a teenager again, I found dating very uncomfortable. Besides, I was still missing Jack, who had once said, "If anything ever happens to me, I hope you will save yourself for someone special." I vowed to do just that. In the meantime, I would enjoy my work, my colleagues, and friends.

Two years later, November 1982, my friend Penny went through the torture of a gastric cancer operation while I endured a hysterectomy during the same week. I improved every day but Penny went downhill. I couldn't believe the change in her personality, and her physiology. She died in the spring after six months of utter agony.

Little did I know that, fifteen years later, I would be diagnosed with the same disease and, as of this writing, by God's grace, I have survived. That experience will be another story in my voyage. When Penny died, my sojourn to the neighborhood hangout also ended.

Life in the apartment complex was not the same and, to make matters worse, the landlord began raising the rent every six months. Although I dearly loved my spacious, two-bedroom, two bath apartment with its beautiful hardwood floors, and within walking distance of the university, I needed to invest my money, not pay rent. In addition, I needed a place on the first floor where Charlie could have access to the out-of-doors.

One of the difficult aspects of moving from the country had been taking my country cat to a second floor apartment. Morning and evening, I carried Charlie down the steps where she navigated the parking lot to the woods and creek behind. She was not a happy camper.

After two years in the apartment, I purchased a first floor condominium and moved again. I would let Charlie out and, thirty minutes later, she was perched on the window ledge wanting to come in. If she could have talked, she might have said, "This is okay Mom; I love you, but where are my country mice and my horses?"

While I had become a city dweller, my haven and weekend retreat continued at the cottage. Charlie did not like to travel, so I usually left her at home when I went to the country.

One particular weekend was a significant and pivotal turning point. Twenty years later, my heart is sad to even think about it. My son and his girl friend, April, had joined me for the weekend.

Yasmin, by then three years old, had been trained by a professional and was ready, I thought, to receive a rider. We saddled the horses. Bill rode Echo and I gingerly placed my foot in the stirrup and climbed on Yasmin's back. She walked a few steps and suddenly, out of nowhere, our neighbor across the road slammed his screen door.

That did it. Yasmin's front hooves rose three feet off the ground. She threw me over her hindquarters and took off. As I lay dazed on the hard ground, wondering if I had broken any bones, Yasmin returned to my side and looked at me as if to say, "What in the world are you doing down there?"

With her aristocratic Arabian head and its white star lowered to my face, her rough tongue licked my cheek. Although she may have been spooked by the sound of the door, I firmly believe she was exerting the only power she had over her mistress. Yasmin was an intelligent horse and may have punished me for sending her away to be trained. Whatever the reason, my head was dealt a terrific blow.

Returning to the cottage with April's help, I felt as if the whole world had gone catawampus. My brain cells were spinning and my childhood flashed before my eyes like a movie reel in fast forward motion. The swelling on my head gradually subsided, following the application of an ice pack, and slowly my surroundings came into focus.

After taking the horses back to the barn, Bill called Dr. Walter Chess, our family physician, who agreed to see me at his office. Doc Chess was a giant of a man at six-feet-eight inches tall, and his hands were the size of a catcher's mitt. In spite of his intimidating frame, Walter was a gentle person who cared deeply about his friends. A committed and loyal member of Muskingum's board, he and Jack had a fond and mutual respect for each other.

Although no bones appeared to be broken, I had dislocated a joint on the third finger of my left hand. For several weeks, I wore a splint on my finger, but the joint remains crooked to this day. Years later, after having a PET scan, I was told that a small stroke had occurred some time in my life. The fall from my horse was no doubt the cause. The unfortunate experience of being thrown turned out to be a pivotal and deciding moment in my life. I have not been on a horse from that day until this. What a mistake.

Echo and Yasmin needed to be groomed, exercised, and ridden daily. I was no longer there for them. Deep in my heart,

I knew that I had to let go in order to move on. Several months later, I sold my horses to an Arabian breeder who lived south of Zanesville. Her name was Carolyn.

Early one Saturday morning, I groomed my horses for the last time. The tears gushed as my favorite pets were herded into Carolyn's horse trailer for the ride to their new home. Echo and Yasmin had been my buddies during the saddest period of my life. Initially, I expected that I might visit them at the Arabian horse farm, but I never did. It would have been too painful. Twenty years later, while writing this book, without warning, I cried. I thought about my horses and wondered if they were still alive.

As the horse trailer drove out of sight that morning, I suddenly realized that another chapter in my life was over. I wondered what the next stage would reveal. Taking one day at a time, I enjoyed my condominium, the special relationship I shared with my son, my colleagues and friends, and my challenging job.

My work at the university fulfilled my passion to write and to travel. Most of my forays took me to cities in Ohio and Michigan, but occasionally I visited private foundations in New York, Washington, Chicago, or Los Angeles.

Although I missed Jack, as the old saying goes, "I was foot-loose and fancy-free." I thoroughly enjoyed my freedom and savored my independent life style. I was alone, but never lonely. Like glorious dreams, I treasured my memories, and my faith sustained me.

Remarriage was the farthest thought from my mind. I had been spoiled rotten by Jack Brown, and had yet to meet anyone who measured up to the standards that I had come to expect. My position at the university included an adequate salary and a generous pension plan and thus, I felt perfectly capable of supporting myself. If I should become strapped for money, there were options. I could rent or sell the farm. I could also sell my condominium and rent an apartment.

Now and then, these thoughts moved in and out of my consciousness. And then, unexpectedly one day, I met Nicholas John Perrini—a man who would become my partner for the rest of my life.

For four years I had been table hopping at lunch with historians, scientists, musicians, lawyers, and nurses. One lunch time in 1984, I joined a table of music professors. I had admired Nicholas, better known as Nick, from afar as he conducted the university's orchestra, but this was our first face-to-face encounter. Why it had taken so long for us to meet is a mystery.

After thirty minutes of lively conversation, most of the professors at the table left for their one o'clock classes. Nick seemed in no rush, so we continued chatting. He had the most beautiful, thick shock of white hair I had ever seen, and his eyes were dark, sparkling like black diamonds. Much to my surprise, a week later he called and invited me to dinner at Fisherman's Wharf which, in later years, would become one of our favorite haunts.

Nicholas John Perrini
(*photo courtesy Dr. John Geisler*)

That first evening, the conversation was lively while we enjoyed a dinner of shrimp cocktail, filet of Dover sole, and a bottle of white burgundy from eastern France. I soon learned that Nick was an amateur winemaker when he's not making music.

Although his first passion was teaching students at Capital's Conservatory of Music, not far behind was his love for the French horn. For thirty-six years, Nick had two full-time jobs: first chair horn of the Columbus Symphony Orchestra, and a professor at Capital which included teaching horn, music theory and history, and conducting the university's orchestra.

Nick was not only knowledgeable, interesting, and an articulate conversationalist, but he was charming, fun to be with, and treated me with respect. I was impressed, and he appeared to enjoy my company, as well. Nick had been divorced for several years and seemed hungry for companionship, as was I.

On the other hand, I don't believe either of us thought our

friendship would lead to marriage. We were both very different from each other. Nick's momentum overflowed with nervous energy, while I was calm and laid back. He was a night person, while I was ready to sleep by eleven. But, the old adage "opposites attract" prevailed.

An unexpected and glorious relationship began on that long ago evening at Fisherman's Wharf. Sandwiched between musical concerts and my work and travel, Nick and I saw each other as our schedules allowed.

After several months of dinners, luncheons, and movies, summer was over and it was time for the fall semester to begin. Suddenly, my phone was soundless. Perhaps, I thought, he had escaped to some other friend, or else dropped off the face of the earth, or maybe he was just busy with the opening weeks of school. I didn't even see him strolling across the campus, or dining at the faculty club. When the silence continued, I concluded that I must have said something that caused him to shy away from a closer relationship.

Even though Jack had been gone almost seven years, I was not ready to pursue any liasion beyond friendship. Nick Perrini had become an important friend and I enjoyed his companionship, so I did hope that he might call again.

In the meantime, I had become increasingly involved with several volunteer activities, and was spending less and less time at my place in the country. I also was paying on two mortgages, and concluded that I needed some financial relief; thus, I came to another important decision.

Although my heart skipped a beat every time I thought about it, I knew that it was time to consider renting my cottage. Hopefully, I would find someone who would take good care of it. But before advertising, I had to either sell or give away the barrage of accumulated stuff that I no longer used or needed.

It was time to have another garage sale, but this time I would be on my own. Jack and I had held a garage sale before moving to Ohio. Using a wonderful little book by James Michael Ullman, *How to Hold a Garage Sale*, we'd organized a rousing success. Although such a task was more than I wanted to undertake single-handedly, I knew that it had to be done.

In August and September, I spent most weekends at the farm getting ready for an October garage sale. Again using Ullman's book as my guide, household items, hundred of books, old LIFE and National Geographic magazines, select pieces of furniture, and old tools were priced and labeled, one by one. Although some items were difficult to part with, I included a few antiques as well as some silver pieces and china to attract buyers. Thank goodness Bill was able to help with this undertaking before he returned to college. Without him, the sale could never have come to fruition.

By early October, every square inch of the make-shift tables that had been erected in the garage were filled and overflowed to the concrete floor beneath. I placed advertisements in the New Concord, Cambridge, and Zanesville newspapers.

Throngs of people arrived on the normally quiet country road more than an hour before the scheduled time of nine o'clock. Two days later, with more than a thousand dollars to supplement my bank account, I was exhausted, but happy. I locked the garage door and headed my Ford Fiesta in a westerly direction. How I navigated to my condo with my aching muscles and tired body, I'll never know.

An hour-and-a-half later, as I unlocked the door to my condo, the telephone was ringing. I thought that I was too tired to talk with anyone, until I heard the voice on the other end of the line. It was Nick inviting me to dinner that evening at the Bombay Bicycle Club. Tired or not, I was glad to hear from him and accepted his surprise invitation. Invigorated by a shower, change of clothes, and freshly applied make-up, I was ready when the doorbell rang.

Dinner was somewhat awkward. I, of course, with the curiosity of a cat, wanted to know where he had been, but that information was not forthcoming, and I did not ask. Upon reflection, I think perhaps he had been playing games and wanted to see how I would react. Frankly, I was so turned on by my winning garage sale that I probably wasn't sensitive to what had been going on with him. Besides, I had never been a game player, and didn't intend to start at approaching middle age.

Once Nick and I moved beyond the initial uneasiness, we were back in the swing of seeing each other at least twice a week. More often than not, after symphony concerts, we took a late night swim in the condominium pool, then shared supper by candlelight. I relished those evenings and, at last, I had someone to cook for again. Nick enjoyed good food and appreciated creative cooking.

After we had been dating for almost a year, I vividly remember a special occasion preceding an outdoor summer concert of the Columbus Symphony. We enjoyed an early supper of shrimp salad at my place. Nick was exceptionally quiet, then suddenly he uttered the unexpected, "Will you marry me?" I was absolutely stunned. My tummy flip-flopped as if I were turning a somersault. I wasn't ready for such a startling proposal. And, I didn't know if I was ready to remarry.

After living alone for eight years, much to my surprise, I believed that I loved Nicholas Perrini. But, was I ready for the awesome responsibilities of another marriage? Couldn't we just continue as we were?

My ancestors would be horrified at the thought that one of their own had had three husbands, I thought, or would they? My grandfather Alvis was twice a widower and my grandmother was his third wife. No doubt my son and my parents would be shocked initially. At the same time, I knew they would be happy for me.

Nick clasped my hands and I looked into his coal-black eyes. We kissed, and I said, "Yes, I will marry you."

Later, as the evening sun glowed on the horizon and I listened to the music at the Columbus Symphony Pops Concert, I pinched myself. Was Nick's proposal real, or was I dreaming? My heart trembled with happiness as the music soared in the heavens. I knew Jack Brown was up there somewhere beaming with pride. Yes, Jack, I saved myself for someone extra special.

And thus was launched the most artistic, adventuresome, and exciting voyage of my life. We were married on Labor Day weekend, August 29, 1985, at Christ Lutheran Church, with my boss, The Reverend Harvey Stegemoeller, officiating, and Nick's horn choir providing the music. Nick's mother, brother, sister-in-law, my parents, our children, and families were present for the celebration and the reception and dinner

Nick and Nancy

which followed at the Berwick Party House.

We spent the night at what would become my future home and, the next morning, departed for our honeymoon hotel in Cincinnati. After two short days, we returned to Columbus and were back to work on Tuesday morning.

I moved into Nick's sprawling split level house, and sold my condominium several weeks later. Once again, I had glorious space, a home and kitchen designed for entertaining, and Charlie was ecstatic to romp in the green grass, climb trees, and chase wild animals again. Although there have been renovations and additions, we continue to live in the same home, twenty years later. The only thing missing is Charlie, who died at the age of nineteen. We miss her still.

Although Nick and I have endured the trials and tribulations of any marriage, including an incredible battle with metastatic adenocarcinoma, our love and commitment to each other have woven a beautiful tapestry far beyond my greatest expectations.

From my childhood, I loved music, took piano lessons, and sang in the church choir, but since our marriage, music has been implanted on my soul as a necessary part of my existence, along with a passion for writing, ballroom dancing, and a little golf for exercise and fun.

After nineteen years of drafting proposals and raising dollars for Capital University, I retired, and now devote the better part of each day to the process of writing what I want to write. If I'm not doing it, I'm thinking about it—all the time. It is an obsession.

Nick continues his love of teaching, conducting his orchestra, and playing the horn. Life is rich with symphonic concerts, operas, theater, dancing, and travels in North America, as well as Europe.

Until 1990, travel in Europe was only an unfulfilled dream for me. Nick had spent two years in Germany as an officer in the U.S. Army's Sixth Armored Cavalry Regiment, but never had been to his native country of Italy.

Over the past thirteen years, we have crossed the Atlantic nine times round trip, and traversed the peaks and valleys of eastern and western Europe, from England south to Greece and east to a small village in Hungary, where we spent two weeks with Capital students at the Kodaly Institute. Our favorite countries are France and Italy, where we love the food, the culture, and the people.

Throughout our marriage, Nick and I have been blessed with the love and support of our families. My parents welcomed Nick into the family, and my father was particularly delighted the first time he was called "Pop." While Nick's father was deceased before we met, his mother was ecstatic when we married. Until her death, we dined together every Sunday.

Mom Perrini taught me how to cook Italian, and hundreds of Capital students have enjoyed her heritage. Nick's two daughters, Justine and Elisa, their husbands, and five grandchildren have brought much happiness to our busy lives.

Nick and grandchildren

Regrettably, my dear mother and first role model died of multiple myeloma early in my marriage to Nick and, five years later, my dad joined her.

Bill, who is blessed with many of his grandfather's characteristics, found the love of his life and married his high school classmate, Christina Lynn Miller. Christy was a student at Muskingum when we lived in New Concord.

Bill and Christy have brought special joy and happiness to each other, as well as to Nick and me. Their support during my bout with cancer has been unbelievable. In addition, their union has further cemented the Muskingum connection with many friendships and wonderful memories.

Bill and Christy

David and Katie moved to Alabama where they raised two boys, John Anthony Brown, III and Zachary Philip Brown. Regrettably, after twenty-five years of marriage, David and Katie separated and divorced. Tragically, two years later, following triple-bypass surgery, David suffered cardiac arrest and died on December 30, 2004. David will be missed, but I will treasure the memories, and the relationship with Katie, John, and Zack will carry on.

Although memories of Jack flash in and out of my consciousness, they flood me with joy and gratitude. Like an unexpected song, sometimes his spirit appears out of nowhere, cheering me on.

Five years after Nick and I married, I sold the cottage, but I often think it would be a great spot for my writing and for Nick's fishing. The latest owners have taken exceptional care of the property, added a screened porch, and built a new barn. Who knows? When Nick retires, maybe we'll repurchase the property, have a pond excavated, and stock it with bass.

And so this odyssey, with all the joys, sorrows, and dreams coming full circle, must close, but God's glorious sun will rise again tomorrow as another story enfolds.

"Love will always ask a great price from us, but it is such a glorious blessing."

Nick and Nancy (with Barry)
at the Matterhorn,
Zermatt, Switzerland.

ABOUT THE AUTHOR

Nancy Brown Perrini, M.A. is a professional writer and development officer with thirty-three years' experience in higher education. A writer for a liberal arts college and for a private university, she co-authored an academic paper, edited a weekly newspaper column, and wrote more than nine hundred grant proposals. Her writing expertise developed during undergraduate/graduate school and through on-the-job experience.

Early in her career Perrini worked for Barnes Hospital, St. Louis, Missouri, as an EKG technician and was also a librarian in the radiology department at Washington University Medical School. As a consultant, she reorganized scheduling procedures in the radiology department at St. Luke's Hospital, St. Louis.

Receiving a B.A. degree in psychology from Lindenwood College, St. Charles, Missouri, she later became alumnae director, dean of students, and director of admissions at her alma mater. Writing and organizational skills were essential to her success in daily correspondence and in the development of brochures and newsletters to constituents.

Following her husband as he became president of Muskingum College in Ohio, she advanced her writing career as editor for "As an Educator Sees It" by Anthony Brown, published weekly in the Daily Jeffersonian, Cambridge, Ohio. After her husband's death, she enrolled in graduate school at The Ohio State University, receiving her M.A. in higher education administration. She was hired by Capital University, Columbus, Ohio where she served as director of corporate/foundation relations for nineteen years. Her writing skills were instrumental in raising capital, endowment, and special project funds for the university.

Upon her retirement in 1999, Perrini was awarded the distinction of Honorary Alumnus of Capital University and was honored by the Council for the Advancement and Support of Education, (CASE), the Independent College Advancement Association, (ICAA), and the Ohio

Foundation of Independent Colleges, (OFIC). During her tenure at Capital she was a conference presenter for CASE and ICAA conferences and a volunteer field representative for OFIC. Throughout her career she was a presenter at workshops hosted by the Columbus Metropolitan Library, The Grantsmanship Center, Hugh O'Brien Youth Foundation, Ohio Parent-Teacher's Association, Ohio Federation on Aging Research, and the American Lutheran Church's annual Dean's Conference. She taught proposal writing workshops for university faculty and also imparted her knowledge of grant writing to students in social work classes.

Credentials include recognition in Who's Who of American Women and Outstanding Young Women of America. Board memberships include: the Board of Directors of the Central Ohio Chapter, National Society of Fundraising Executives; the Southeastern Ohio Symphony Orchestra; and Stuart Pimsler Dance & Theater. Currently, Perrini's volunteer activities focus on a not-for-profit private foundation, the Women's Fund of Central Ohio, and her church, where she serves as a lector.

Printed in the United States
26378LVS00002B/1-80